JOSEPH DUREPOS

D0631716

2024
A BOOK OF GRACE-FILLED DAYS

LOYOLA PRESS.
A JESUIT MINISTRY
Chicago

LOYOLA PRESS.
A JESUIT MINISTRY

www.loyolapress.com

Cover and interior design by Kathy Kikkert.

ISBN: 978-0-8294-5513-7

Printed in the United States of America.
23 24 25 26 27 28 29 30 31 32 Lake Book 10 9 8 7 6 5 4 3 2 1

INTRODUCTION

Christmas of 1963. I was eight years old, it was bitterly cold, and I had tired of playing with the toys I received for Christmas. The snow was piled so high, my mother told me to find something to do inside. Other than some new socks, all that remained for me under the tree were a couple of books: the first two Hardy Boys mysteries. I approached them with resigned indifference.

I opened the first book, and my life changed forever. I became a reader. I discovered that living in a story could feel more real than playing outside with friends. I learned that through story we engage a part of ourselves that otherwise lies dormant.

The Bible at its heart is a story and, as with any good story, it's easy to get caught up in it. There are wars, times of peace, great moments of sacrifice and courage, and bewildering acts of cruelty and betrayal. The Bible is as real and relatable as the evening news.

The Church boiled all this story-telling down into a collection of Daily Readings in the Lectionary. These stories are central to our faith. They are the narrative of our faith journey from the Old Testament through the New.

The reflections in this book are the fruit of my year-long deep dive into the Daily Readings. Read them, and then read the passages they are based on. If you do that, I think it very likely that you will experience a profound journey. Here are just a few things that stood out for me.

- The humanity of Jesus is astounding. Think about it: *God was a human being like us!*
- God goes to great lengths to reassure us not to be afraid.
- God promises he will always be with us.
- God chooses flawed, imperfect people to perform unimaginably great and transformative feats. He may choose you, too.
- Love is at the heart of all things.

I also learned that I'm a participant in this story, this epic tale of a loving God reaching out to his chosen people. The story is still unfolding, and we are now the chosen people. Your part in the story is important; it's your response to God's call. Let this humble volume help you on your journey.

Sunday

DECEMBER 3

• FIRST SUNDAY OF ADVENT •

[Jesus said to his disciples,]
"Be watchful! Be alert!
You do not know when the time will come."
—MARK 13:33

I wonder if, rather than a stern admonition from Jesus, this is meant as a gentle reminder, an encouragement to be mindful and aware, always. Often we are told to "pay attention!" but not always with sufficient encouragement or explanation.

What if Jesus is suggesting that the reason for being watchful, for being aware, is that we don't miss the arrival of something wonderful?—the very definition of Advent.

Isaiah 63:16b–17,19b; 64:2–7
Psalm 80:2–3,15–16,18–19 (4)
1 Corinthians 1:3–9
Mark 13:33–37

⇒ 1 ⇐

DECEMBER 4

• ST. JOHN DAMASCENE, PRIEST AND DOCTOR OF THE CHURCH •

The centurion said in reply,
"Lord, I am not worthy to have you enter under my roof;
only say the word and my servant will be healed."
—MATTHEW 8:8

It is extraordinary to realize that this beautiful prayer of brokenness and humility we say together before receiving the Eucharist at Mass derives from the words of a Roman centurion. Upon encountering Jesus, he beseeches him to come to his home and heal one of his servants. The centurion is a man of power, but also a pagan, a despised Roman, and yet he truly recognizes Jesus for who he is and knows that Jesus can heal his servant. This Advent season, let us have the faith of that centurion: "Lord, I am not worthy to have you enter under my roof; but only say the word and my soul shall be healed."

Isaiah 2:1–5
Psalm 122:1–2,3–4b,4cd–5,6–7,8–9
Matthew 8:5–11

DECEMBER 5

[Jesus] rejoiced in the Holy Spirit and said,
"I give you praise, Father, Lord of heaven and earth,
for although you have hidden these things
from the wise and the learned
you have revealed them to the childlike.
Yes, Father, such has been your gracious will."
—LUKE 10:21

It's clear in this passage from Luke, and elsewhere in
Scripture, that Jesus is letting us know we will not always
understand the nature of God through our intelligence. But
when we look at Jesus, what do we see? We see love. We see
a glimpse of the reality of what God is. We see what *we* can
be. How? Not by being clever but by being as loving as
Jesus. Love—it's that simple. So simple a child
can understand.

Isaiah 11:1–10
Psalm 72:1–2,7–8,12–13,17
Luke 10:21–24

Jesus summoned his disciples and said,
"My heart is moved with pity for the crowd,
for they have been with me now for three days
and have nothing to eat.
I do not want to send them away hungry,
for fear they may collapse on the way."
—MATTHEW 15:32

All three readings today remind us of a startling and remarkable fact of our faith: God's endless generosity. In the reading from Matthew, we find Jesus, after three days of healing and teaching, no doubt exhausted from the exertion of tending to four thousand people—but concerned most that the multitudes have something to eat so they can journey back to their homes, not only with spirits inspired, hearts on fire, but also with bellies full. This is our God.

Isaiah 25:6–10a
Psalm 23:1–3a,3b–4,5,6
Matthew 15:29–37

DECEMBER 7

Give thanks to the LORD, for he is good,
for his mercy endures forever.
—PSALM 118:1

The world can seem a broken place, our lives sometimes
marked by tragedy and sadness. But we also know how
powerful a timely act of goodness or mercy can be, like a
pebble dropped into a still pond, with ripples reaching the
far shorelines. This Advent, let us remember that the Christ
child is that pebble. Let us celebrate his arrival by reaching
out to those around us with acts of goodness and mercy. For
God has come among us, and his enduring graces are
rippling ever outward.

Isaiah 26:1–6
Psalm 118:1 and 8–9,19–21,25–27a
Matthew 7:21,24–27

DECEMBER 8

• THE IMMACULATE CONCEPTION OF THE BLESSED VIRGIN MARY
(PATRONAL FEAST DAY OF THE UNITED STATES OF AMERICA) •

*Then the angel said to her,
"Do not be afraid, Mary,
for you have found favor with God."*
—LUKE 1:30

Mary's yes to the angel sets in motion the events that are at the heart of our great Advent mystery. A scared, poor, uneducated teenage girl, living in a small town, is chosen by God to be the vessel of his child. A child who came into our world and transformed it with justice, love, peace, and salvation. A child who forever changed history and continues to change it still. But it all began when a frightened young girl had the courage to say yes to the angel of God.

Genesis 3:9–15,20
Psalm 98:1,2–3ab,3cd–4
Ephesians 1:3–6,11–12
Luke 1:26–38

DECEMBER 9

• ST. JUAN DIEGO CUAUHTLATOATZIN, HERMIT •

[Jesus said,] "Without cost you have received; without cost you are to give."
—MATTHEW 10:8

Jesus has commissioned the twelve disciples to go out into all the towns and villages and proclaim that the kingdom of heaven is at hand. He has instructed them to cure every disease and every illness, but as they go, he reminds them from whence their power comes—not from them but through them—from the Father above. This is grace, God acting in the world.

Isaiah 30:19–21,23–26
Psalm 147:1–2,3–4,5–6
Matthew 9:35—10:1,5a,6–8

Sunday

DECEMBER 10

• SECOND SUNDAY OF ADVENT •

[Jesus said,] "I have baptized you with water;
he will baptize you with the Holy Spirit."
—MARK 1:8

These are the words of John the Baptist, preparing us for the
promise of Advent, the arrival of Jesus. John's baptism is one
of repentance. It is the forgiveness of our sins in readiness for
an entirely different kind of baptism. Jesus tells us that unless
we are born again, we cannot see the kingdom of God. This
is the baptism of the Spirit, the benediction of beginning
again, like the first morning of creation. All is cleansed, all is
waiting in the vast still silence of the purest absolution. As St.
Paul writes, "The old has gone, the new is here!"
(2 Corinthians 5:17).

Isaiah 40:1–5,9–11
Psalm 85:9–10,11–12,13–14 (8)
2 Peter 3:8–14
Mark 1:1–8

⇒ 8 ⇐

DECEMBER 11

• ST. DAMASUS I, POPE •

When Jesus saw their faith, he said,
"As for you, your sins are forgiven."
—LUKE 5:20

A group of men lower a paralyzed man through a hole in the roof of the house where Jesus is teaching. Jesus heals the paralyzed man and tells him, "I say to you, rise, pick up your stretcher, and go home." Jesus "saw their faith"—a faith that prompts people to scramble onto a roof, cut a hole in it, and lower another person into a house. This is faith that moves from hope to trust, from trust to surrender, from surrender to forgiveness, from forgiveness to healing, and finally to a complete restoration of wholeness. We should never underestimate the power of faith.

Isaiah 35:1–10
Psalm 85:9ab and 10,11–12,13–14
Luke 5:17–26

Mary said, "Behold, I am the handmaid of the Lord.
May it be done to me according to your word."
Then the angel departed from her.
—LUKE 1:38

Mary is confused and more than a little worried about all that
the angel has told her concerning her coming pregnancy and
the pregnancy of her elderly cousin Elizabeth. And yet how
does she respond? "Behold, I am the handmaid of the Lord.
May it be done to me according to your word." Mary's
response to the angel is a beautiful prayer. Rev. Paul David
Tripp in *New Morning Mercies* writes, "True prayer happens at
the intersection of surrender and celebration." That sounds
exactly like what we see in Mary: prayer, surrender,
and celebration.

Zechariah 2:14–17 or Revelation 11:19a; 12:1–6a,10ab
Judith 13:18bcde,19
Luke 1:26–38 or 1:39–47
or any readings from the Common of the Blessed Virgin Mary

Wednesday

DECEMBER 13

• ST. LUCY, VIRGIN AND MARTYR •

"Come to me, all you who labor and are burdened,
and I will give you rest.
Take my yoke upon you and learn from me,
for I am meek and humble of heart;
and you will find rest for yourselves.
For my yoke is easy, and my burden light."
—MATTHEW 11:28–30

A yoke is a heavy collar, like those worn by a beast of burden, or perhaps like those burdens we bear in life. But what is the yoke of Jesus? It's love, immeasurable and unconditional. What is the burden of Jesus? It's light, to be the light in the darkness. As we move through the Advent mystery, we acknowledge that our burdens become bearable while our paths become lit by the light of the coming Lord.

Isaiah 40:25–31
Psalm 103:1–2,3–4,8 and 10
Matthew 11:28–30

DECEMBER 14

• ST. JOHN OF THE CROSS, PRIEST AND DOCTOR OF THE CHURCH •

Your Kingdom is a Kingdom for all ages,
and your dominion endures through all generations.
—PSALM 145:13A

As Christians we believe there is more than the here and
now, more than the present moment. We believe in eternity,
one we are always moving toward, or away from. And how
we live now will affect how we live in eternity. Each moment,
we have a choice to choose God, and draw closer to an
eternity of love in the fullness of creation. That is the reality
of the present moment, extending into eternity, but hinging
on the choice we make in the here and now.

Isaiah 41:13–20
Psalm 145:1 and 9,10–11,12–13ab
Matthew 11:11–15

*"The Son of Man came eating and drinking and they said,
'Look, he is a glutton and a drunkard,
a friend of tax collectors and sinners.'
But wisdom is vindicated by her works."*
—MATTHEW 11:19

This is a difficult passage. Jesus is saying to the crowds that
they're like children who have watched and heard John the
Baptist and Jesus himself, and somehow missed their message
and their works. The people failed to understand who John
and Jesus were or recognize the kingdom they were
proclaiming. Let's not miss the Lord when he is with us; let's
not miss the message of his ministers who proclaim his
kingdom as John did for Jesus. God is present for those who
look and see. This Advent, perhaps our prayer might simply
be, "Lord, let me not miss you!"

Isaiah 48:17–19
Psalm 1:1–2,3,4 and 6
Matthew 11:16–19

DECEMBER 16

May your help be with the man of your right hand,
with the son of man whom you yourself made strong.
Then we will no more withdraw from you;
give us new life, and we will call upon your name.
—PSALM 80:18–19

This psalm dates to approximately eight hundred to nine hundred years before the time of Jesus, or roughly three thousand years ago. Almost all biblical commentary affirms that the "son of man" referred to here is indeed Jesus. We feel the profound longing in the heart of God's people, over the centuries, awaiting the birth of the coming Messiah. A longing now fulfilled and celebrated in this the Advent season.

Sirach 48:1–4,9–11
Psalm 80:2ac and 3b,15–16,18–19
Matthew 17:9a,10–13

DECEMBER 17

Rejoice always. Pray without ceasing.
In all circumstances give thanks,
for this is the will of God for you in Christ Jesus.
—1 THESSALONIANS 5:16–18

As we move through Advent, the words of St. Paul encourage us to "pray without ceasing" and "in all circumstances give thanks." And we do this because we know something glorious is at hand. The coming of Emmanuel: God with us. A mystery so profound, only faith can comprehend it. The popular traditional Christmas hymn "O Holy Night" features the soaring refrain "Fall on your knees . . ." As we prepare for the birth of the Christ child, we may find ourselves wanting to do just that—fall on our knees, rejoice, and pray without ceasing, for our Lord is coming.

Isaiah 61:1–2a,10–11
Luke 1:46–48,49–50,53–54
1 Thessalonians 5:16–24
John 1:6–8,19–28

Joseph her husband, since he was a righteous man,
yet unwilling to expose her to shame,
decided to divorce her quietly.
Such was his intention when, behold,
the angel of the Lord appeared to him in a dream and said,
"Joseph, son of David,
do not be afraid to take Mary your wife into your home.
For it is through the Holy Spirit
that this child has been conceived in her."
—MATTHEW 1:19–20

When I consider what Joseph was going through during this
tumultuous time of Mary's pregnancy, and later the events
surrounding the birth of Jesus, I sense Joseph's complete and
utter trust in a mystery so profound he couldn't begin to
understand it. But whatever burning questions Joseph had in
his heart, the answer was always the same: trust in the Lord.

Jeremiah 23:5–8
Psalm 72:1–2,12–13,18–19
Matthew 1:18–25

DECEMBER 19

Then Zechariah said to the angel,
"How shall I know this?
For I am an old man, and my wife is advanced in years."
And the angel said to him in reply,
"I am Gabriel, who stand before God.
I was sent to speak to you and to announce to you this good news.
But now you will be speechless and unable to talk
until the day these things take place,
because you did not believe my words,
which will be fulfilled at their proper time."
—LUKE 1:18–20

Zechariah was a priest, a man of great faith. But when a
miracle occurred in his life and an angel appeared to him,
announced the miracle, and explained it to him, he could not
accept it. Let us pray that our faith allows us to accept the
miraculous when it occurs in our lives.

Judges 13:2–7,24–25a
Psalm 71:3–4a,5–6ab,16–17
Luke 1:5–25

DECEMBER 20

And coming to her, [the angel] said,
"Hail, full of grace! The Lord is with you."
But she was greatly troubled at what was said
and pondered what sort of greeting this might be.
—LUKE 1:27–28

There is a famous prayer by Blessed Charles de Foucauld (1858–1916) that begins with these words: "Father, I abandon myself into your hands; do with me what you will. Whatever you may do, I thank you; I am ready for all, I accept all." When I think of Mary, young and inexperienced, and hearing the startling words of the angel Gabriel, "greatly troubled" might be an understatement. But perhaps with the angel's reassurance to not be afraid, Mary, like Blessed Charles, could say, "Father, I abandon myself into your hands; do with me what you will."

Isaiah 7:10–14
Psalm 24:1–2,3–4ab,5–6
Luke 1:26–38

DECEMBER 21

• ST. PETER CANISIUS, PRIEST AND DOCTOR OF THE CHURCH •

Our soul waits for the LORD,
who is our help and our shield,
For in him our hearts rejoice;
in his holy name we trust.
—PSALM 33:20–21

We learn over time that being happy is not the absence of trouble; it's rather the strength to persevere when trouble comes, because it will. When Psalm 33 says the Lord is "our help and our shield," the psalmist is reminding us that with God we can do what we cannot do alone, for God's strength becomes our strength.

Song of Songs 2:8–14 or Zephaniah 3:14–18a
Psalm 33:2–3,11–12,20–21
Luke 1:39–45

*"The Almighty has done great things for me,
and holy is his Name."*
—LUKE 1:49

In the film series *The Chosen*, there is a scene included in the longer Christmas event shown in theaters during Advent 2021. Mary, toward the end of her life, summons Mary Magdalene to her bedside. She wants Luke to have something for the account of Jesus he's writing. Mary reads it aloud; it is the Magnificat, in all its beauty. Mary Magdalene begins to cry tears of joy and wonder at what she's hearing. She's not the only one; people throughout the theater reached for their tissues as we also heard those beautiful words: "My soul proclaims the greatness of the Lord; my spirit rejoices in God my savior."

1 Samuel 1:24–28
1 Samuel 2:1,4–5,6–7,8abcd
Luke 1:46–56

When they came on the eighth day to circumcise the child,
they were going to call him Zechariah after his father,
but his mother said in reply,
"No. He will be called John."
—LUKE 1:59–60

I'm struck by how calmly Elizabeth appears to accept all that happens. She accepts that if God chooses a woman past child-bearing years to bear a healthy son, then she will. If an angel of the Lord tells her niece Mary, an unmarried virgin, that she is pregnant, then it must be so. And when it comes to her own child, if God wants to break with long-standing family naming traditions and give that child a name, then so be it. Elizabeth takes everything in calm equanimity, trusting the Lord with unwavering faith.

Malachi 3:1–4,23–24
Psalm 25:4–5ab,8–9,10 and 14
Luke 1:57–66

DECEMBER 24

Brothers and sisters:
To him who can strengthen you,
according to my gospel and the proclamation of Jesus Christ,
according to the revelation of the mystery kept secret for long ages
—ROMANS 16:25

I am a serious reader of mysteries. I especially love Sherlock Holmes, who famously said, "When you have eliminated all which is impossible, then whatever remains, however improbable, must be the truth." On Christmas Eve, as we prepare for the culminating mystery of Advent, we pause and notice that a certain calm settles upon us after the crush of getting ready for Christmas Day. This seems impossible, given the frenzy of the holiday season. And yet, there is that moment of quiet certainty that something momentous, something miraculous, however improbable, is about to occur.

2 Samuel 7:1–5,8b–12,14a,16
Psalm 89:2–3,4–5,27,29 (2a)
Romans 16:25–27
Luke 1:26–38

DECEMBER 25

• THE NATIVITY OF THE LORD (CHRISTMAS) •

Beloved:
The grace of God has appeared, saving all.
—TITUS 2:11

On this day, we give thanks for the God who came to us in the guise of a vulnerable babe, born in the humblest of circumstances. A child who became a bridge between the now and the not-yet. A promise fulfilled by a God who does not give up on his people.

The King of kings lay thus in lowly manger
In all our trials, born to be our friend.
He knows our need, to our weakness is no stranger
Behold your King, before him lowly bend.
from "O Holy Night"

VIGIL:	DAWN:
Isaiah 62:1–5	Isaiah 62:11–12
Psalm 89:4–5,16–17,27,29 (2a)	Psalm 97:1,6,11–12
Acts 13:16–17,22–25	Titus 3:4–7
Matthew 1:1–25 or 1:18–25	Luke 2:15–20

NIGHT:	DAY:
Isaiah 9:1–6	Isaiah 52:7–10
Psalm 96:1–2,2–3,11–12,13	Psalm 98:1,2–3,3–4,5–6 (3c)
Titus 2:11–14	Hebrews 1:1–6
Luke 2:1–14	John 1:1–18

DECEMBER 26

• ST. STEPHEN, THE FIRST MARTYR •

*As they were stoning Stephen, he called out,
"Lord Jesus, receive my spirit."*
—ACTS 7:59

As a child, I was frightened more than inspired by the stories
of the martyrs. As a young adult, I began to understand
something of the passions that led the martyrs to acts of
heroic bravery on behalf of their beliefs. As an older adult,
I've come to know the gentleness and compassion of the
Lord I love. I now believe that at the time of our testing, God
gives us assurance of what we cannot see but know to be
true. I believe Stephen knew Jesus was with him in his final,
terrible moments. This is mercy. This is grace.

Acts 6:8–10; 7:54–59
Psalm 31:3cd–4,6 and 8ab,16bc and 17
Matthew 10:17–22

DECEMBER 27

• ST. JOHN, APOSTLE AND EVANGELIST •

We are writing this so that our joy may be complete.
—1 JOHN 1:4

As a lifelong reader and editor, how could I not love John?
He begins his Gospel, "In the beginning was the Word."
John's writings are filled with love and light, joy and
celebration. In fact, John mentions joy two more times in his
letters and seven times in his Gospel. His message seems
clear: God wants us to know joy, and knowing that joy will
make us complete. Today, find a quiet moment to stop and
reflect on joy in your life—that's where you may find God.

1 John 1:1–4
Psalm 97:1–2,5–6,11–12
John 20:1a and 2–8

DECEMBER 28

• THE HOLY INNOCENTS, MARTYRS •

When Herod realized that he had been deceived by the magi,
he became furious.
He ordered the massacre of all the boys in Bethlehem and its vicinity
two years old and under.
—MATTHEW 2:16

This is one of the darkest chapters in the Gospel narratives.
Herod, driven by fear of a potential rival king, even though
only an infant, orders the slaughter of every boy in and
around Bethlehem under the age of two. An unimaginable
horror. The point of the story, however, is God sending an
angel to warn Joseph in a dream, urging him to flee with
Mary and Jesus to Egypt. I'm reminded of a famous quote by
Frederick Buechner: "Here is the world. Beautiful and terrible
things will happen. Don't be afraid."

1 John 1:5—2:2
Psalm 124:2–3,4–5,7cd–8
Matthew 2:13–18

DECEMBER 29

• ST. THOMAS BECKET, BISHOP AND MARTYR •

Jesus said to all,
"Whoever wishes to come after me must deny himself,
take up his cross, and follow me.
For whoever wishes to save his life will lose it,
but whoever loses his life for my sake will find it."
—MATTHEW 16:24–25

What does Jesus mean when he says we must lose our lives
for his sake to find our lives? I'm reminded of the story of the
person cleaning his small fish tank. He takes his fish and
places them in the bathtub. When he finishes cleaning, he
finds the fish have remained in an area roughly the size of
their tank. When we follow Jesus, we leave our small, limited
life behind and find a new life of abundant freedom in
discipleship.

1 John 2:3–11
Psalm 96:1–2a,2b–3,5b–6
Luke 2:22–35

DECEMBER 30

Yet the world and its enticement are passing away.
But whoever does the will of God remains forever.
—1 JOHN 2:17

The Scripture refers to the world's understanding of time, as
well as the reality of God's time. The world's time is always
passing away, but God's time is eternal and never-ending. We
live between the now and the not-yet. Of course, we feel
some tension as we attempt to navigate between these two
realities. Prayer helps us remember that our God is a God of
beginnings and endings and everything in between. Grace
helps us live in the trajectory that stretches into the eternity
of life with God. Faith keeps us on the journey, and love
brings us home to rest in the timeless heart of God.

1 John 2:12–17
Psalm 96:7–8a,8b–9,10
Luke 2:36–40

DECEMBER 31

• THE HOLY FAMILY OF JESUS, MARY, AND JOSEPH •

Now there was a man in Jerusalem whose name was Simeon.
This man was righteous and devout,
awaiting the consolation of Israel,
and the Holy Spirit was upon him.
It had been revealed to him by the Holy Spirit
that he should not see death
before he had seen the Christ of the Lord.
—LUKE 2:25–26

Simeon was promised that before he died he would see the Christ. God kept his promise. Did Simeon make a promise to God? All we are told is that Simeon was a good and righteous man who lived a devout life, and maybe that was Simeon's promise to God.

Genesis 15:1–6; 21:1–3 or Sirach 3:2–6,12–14
Psalm 105:1–2,3–4,5–6,8–9 (7a,8a)
Hebrews 11:8,11–12,17–19 or Colossians 3:12–21 or 3:12–17
Luke 2:22–40 or 2:22, 39–40

⇒ 29 ⇐

Say to [Aaron and his sons]:
The LORD bless you and keep you!
The LORD let his face shine upon you, and be gracious to you!
The LORD look upon you kindly and give you peace!
—NUMBERS 6:23–26

When I was growing up, New Year's Day in my family meant discussions of what generally turned out to be short-lived resolutions. Otherwise, the day was quiet. My dad, my brother, and I watched college football. My mother enjoyed the day with my sisters. These days, I'm older, if not wiser. New Year's Day is even quieter. My only resolution for the new year is the same resolution I make for each new day, to ask the Lord to bless and keep me, to shine his face upon me, and to give me peace.

Numbers 6:22–27
Psalm 67:2–3,5,6,8 (2a)
Galatians 4:4–7
Luke 2:16–21

Tuesday

JANUARY 2

• ST. BASIL THE GREAT AND ST. GREGORY NAZIANZEN, BISHOPS AND
DOCTORS OF THE CHURCH •

He said:
"I am the voice of one crying out in the desert,
'Make straight the way of the Lord,'
as Isaiah the prophet said."
—JOHN 1:23

These are the words of John the Baptist when questioned by
the temple priests and Pharisees, who wanted to know who
he was. Jesus was a carpenter, but we never really learn what
John did for work, for a job. But John knew what his real
work was: he preached the coming of the Messiah. By
baptizing with water, he was preparing the way of the Lord.
We all work, have jobs, and they are important, but let us
remember, like John, that our real work is ushering in the
kingdom of God.

1 John 2:22–28
Psalm 98:1,2–3ab,3cd–4
John 1:19–28

Sing to the LORD a new song.
—PSALM 98:1

This is the day the church celebrates the naming of Jesus.
My mother was very devout, attended daily Mass, prayed,
read Scripture regularly. She went on retreats and had a
spiritual director before it was cool. When I asked her about
prayer, she said all I needed to know was the name of Jesus.
Saying his name was the greatest prayer there was. But that
was way too simple for me. Mom's gone now. The other day
I smiled, thinking of her while driving and listening to
Hillsong United sing "What a Beautiful Name." Indeed, what
a beautiful name it is, the name of Jesus.

1 John 2:29—3:6
Psalm 98:1,3cd–4,5–6
John 1:29–34

Thursday

JANUARY 4

• ST. ELIZABETH ANN SETON, RELIGIOUS •

John was standing with two of his disciples,
and as he watched Jesus walk by, he said,
"Behold, the Lamb of God."
The two disciples heard what he said and followed Jesus.
Jesus turned and saw them following him and said to them,
"What are you looking for?"
They said to him, "Rabbi" (which translated means Teacher),
"where are you staying?"
He said to them, "Come, and you will see."
—JOHN 1:35–39

This Scripture refers to the calling of the first disciples.
Today, wake up and believe that something wonderful will
happen to you. Hold tight to this belief throughout your day.
When it does happen, be grateful. God is good, and God is
calling you to a greater life. "Come, and you will see."

1 John 3:7–10
Psalm 98:1,7–8,9
John 1:35–42

⇒ 33 ⇐

This is the message you have heard from the beginning: we should love one another,
—1 JOHN 3:11

I love a writer's ability to sum up an entire belief system with a brief statement of action, like St. John's last five words in the passage above: "We should love one another."

1 John 3:11–21
Psalm 100:1b–2,3,4,5
John 1:43–51

JANUARY 6

• ST. ANDRÉ BESSETTE, RELIGIOUS •

Beloved:
Who indeed is the victor over the world
but the one who believes that Jesus is the Son of God?
—1 JOHN 5:5

André Bessette (1845–1937) was plagued by ill health much
of his life. As a young man, he became a brother with the
teaching order, the Congregation of the Holy Cross. His
ministry was chiefly that of being door porter at the college
where he lived. Brother André believed that Jesus was the
Son of God and, though André was limited by health
challenges and lack of formal education, he wanted greatly to
share his faith as best he could. He did it by greeting visitors.
Over ten thousand miraculous healings were reported by
those who met the humble porter and shook his hand.

1 John 5:5–13
Psalm 147:12–13,14–15,19–20
Mark 1:7–11 or Luke 3:23–38 or 3:23, 31–34, 36, 38

Behold, magi from the east arrived in Jerusalem saying,
"Where is the newborn king of the Jews?
We saw his star at its rising
and have come to do him homage."
—MATTHEW 2:1–2

I have always been intrigued by the Magi. Who were they? What made them decide to journey so far? Information about them is scant. Basically, they saw a sign, traveled approximately four hundred miles over several weeks through the wilderness, brought gifts, and did homage to a newborn child. Then they traveled home secretly, after which we never hear about them again. Epiphany is defined as something extraordinary breaking through, a shift in reality. It appears that the Magi understood that this child's arrival would change the world.

Isaiah 60:1–6
Psalm 72:1–2,7–8,10–11,12–13
Ephesians 3:2–3a,5–6
Matthew 2:1–12

JANUARY 8

• THE BAPTISM OF THE LORD •

It happened in those days that Jesus came from Nazareth of Galilee
and was baptized in the Jordan by John.
On coming up out of the water he saw the heavens being torn open
and the Spirit, like a dove, descending upon him.
And a voice came from the heavens,
"You are my beloved Son; with you I am well pleased."
—MARK 1:9–11

There are likely many reasons for John's baptism of Jesus.
Jesus affirming John's ministry. Jesus showing the need for
our own baptism. But perhaps most elegant of all, John's
baptism of Jesus is the perfect demonstration of the Holy
Trinity at work. Jesus is baptized, the heavens open, the Holy
Spirit descends, and the Father expresses his love for his Son.

Isaiah 55:1–11 or 1 John 5:1–9
Isaiah 12:2–3,4bcd,5–6 (3)
Mark 1:7–11

Tuesday

JANUARY 9

All were amazed and asked one another,
"What is this?
A new teaching with authority.
He commands even the unclean spirits and they obey him."
His fame spread everywhere throughout the whole region of Galilee.
—MARK 1:27–28

Earlier in Mark we read of Jesus being baptized by John and immediately being driven into the desert for forty days, where he is tempted relentlessly by Satan. Then Jesus begins his teaching in earnest by appearing in a synagogue in Capernaum, where he speaks with great authority and also rebukes and casts out an unclean spirit, who asks, "Have you come to destroy us?" In the beginning of Jesus' public ministry, it appears that Satan and unclean spirits are among the first to recognize who Jesus is and the threat he poses to them. Something to ponder.

1 Samuel 1:9–20
1 Samuel 2:1,4–5,6–7,8abcd
Mark 1:21–28
or 1 Samuel 1:1–8 and 1:9–20/Mark 1:14–20 and 1:21–28

The LORD called to Samuel, who answered, "Here I am."
—1 SAMUEL 3:4

It's worth taking a moment to read the full first Scripture reading for today: 1 Samuel 3:1–10 and 19–20. Then, search online for the article by Colleen Dulle, *"Here I Am, Lord": The Little-Known Story behind a Catholic Hit* (from *America* magazine, October 12, 2017). Finally, find Collin Raye's version of "Here I Am, Lord" on whatever music platform you like and give it a serious listen. From the Scripture reading in Samuel, to the article and the writing of the song, to the recording by Collin Raye—pure inspiration.

1 Samuel 3:1–10,19–20
Psalm 40:2 and 5,7–8a,8b–9,10
Mark 1:29–39

JANUARY 11

The Philistines fought and Israel was defeated;
every man fled to his own tent.
It was a disastrous defeat;
in which Israel lost thirty thousand foot soldiers.
The ark of God was captured.
—1 SAMUEL 4:10–11

The defeat of the Israelites by the Philistines described here is catastrophic. Thirty thousand dead soldiers. The ark of God captured. What are we to draw from a biblical story like this? Perhaps this narrative speaks to the teaching at the core of all Scripture: even when the worst thing possible happens, God can turn it to good. After all, what is the Crucifixion but literally the worst possible thing happening, the Son of God executed like a common criminal? What is the Resurrection? God turning the greatest evil into the greatest good.

1 Samuel 4:1–11
Psalm 44:10–11,14–15,24–25
Mark 1:40–45

JANUARY 12

Blessed the people who know the joyful shout;
in the light of your countenance, O LORD, they walk.
At your name they rejoice all the day,
and through your justice they are exalted.
—PSALM 89:16–17

Psalm 89 is a prayer to the steadfastness of God. It speaks of God's everlasting love for us, and it ends with the beautiful "Blessed be the LORD forever! Amen and amen!" It's good to remember that God is not bound by time. There is no place in our past, present, or future that God was not, is not, or will not be present. So, let the light of God's enduring mercy and healing grace shine into all the secret, broken places of your life. We may be bound by time, but God's transforming love is not.

1 Samuel 8:4–7,10–22a
Psalm 89:16–17,18–19
Mark 2:1–12

Some scribes who were Pharisees saw that Jesus was eating with sinners
and tax collectors and said to his disciples,
"Why does he eat with tax collectors and sinners?"
Jesus heard this and said to them,
"Those who are well do not need a physician, but the sick do.
I did not come to call the righteous but sinners."
—MARK 2:16–17

Clearly, Jesus was not concerned about spending time with
his culture's undesirables. In fact, it often appears that he
sought them out, risking the condemnation of the Pharisees
and others in power. Whatever the conventions of society in
his world, when it came to interacting with people, Jesus'
humanity and basic decency were far greater than any need
for false decorum.

1 Samuel 9:1–4,17–19; 10:1
Psalm 21:2–3,4–5,6–7
Mark 2:13–17

God raised the Lord and will also raise us by his power.
—1 CORINTHIANS 6:14

Coming across an extraordinary line like this one in Scripture, I have to stop and read it several times to grasp the meaning and significance. This is a powerful statement from Paul. It's a foundational belief at the heart of our faith, but it's amazing and hard to take in without serious reflection. Later in this same chapter, Paul writes, "For you have been purchased at a price." That price is Jesus' death on the cross. At a Lenten retreat I attended in 2022, the speaker turned to the crucifix and said, "This is a statement that requires a response." Our response can only be one of unfailing gratitude and wonder.

1 Samuel 3:3b–10,19
Psalm 40:2,4,7–8,8–9,10 (8a,9a)
1 Corinthians 6:13c–15a,17–20
John 1:35–42

⇒ 43 ⇐

JANUARY 15

Likewise, no one pours new wine into old wineskins.
Otherwise, the wine will burst the skins,
and both the wine and the skins are ruined.
Rather, new wine is poured into fresh wineskins.
—MARK 2:22

So, what's the metaphor Jesus offers here? If you want to
search this out, you can go down the same rabbit hole of
scriptural exegesis I've done. Or you can, with a measure of
common sense, read this as Jesus suggesting that a new
message sometimes requires a new container. But how? Here's
the good news: St. Paul writes in 1 Corinthians 5:17,
"Therefore, if anyone is in Christ, the new creation has come.
The old has gone, and the new is here." The transforming
grace of Jesus makes both the wine and the wineskin new.

1 Samuel 15:16–23
Psalm 50:8–9,16bc–17,21 and 23
Mark 2:18–22

JANUARY 16

But the LORD said to Samuel:
"Do not judge from his appearance or from his lofty stature,
because I have rejected him.
Not as man sees does God see,
because he sees the appearance
but the LORD looks into the heart."
—1 SAMUEL 16:7

We should take great comfort from today's Scripture. The Lord does not see us as others see us. The Lord sees into our hearts and sees us as the people we can be. There are no secrets or hidden parts to us that the Lord cannot see. Likewise, when we look at others, we should not judge them upon appearances, for we do not know what is in their hearts, nor do we see their hidden pain or the scars of their great struggles within.

1 Samuel 16:1–13
Psalm 89:20,21–22,27–28
Mark 2:23–28

JANUARY 17

• ST. ANTHONY, ABBOT •

Then he said to the Pharisees,
"Is it lawful to do good on the sabbath rather than to do evil,
to save life rather than to destroy it?"
But they remained silent.
Looking around at them with anger
and grieved at their hardness of heart.
—MARK 3:4–5A

What strikes me when I read this passage is the phrase "and grieved at their hardness of heart." Here were religious leaders in the community who cared more for preserving the law than they did preserving the care and well-being of people. Even though this story is early in Jesus' public ministry, we can already sense the weariness he must have felt, continually coming up against this resistance to his message of love being greater than the law.

1 Samuel 17:32–33,37,40–51
Psalm 144:1b,2,9–10
Mark 3:1–6

JANUARY 18

Now I know that God is with me.
In God, in whose promise I glory,
in God I trust without fear;
—PSALM 56:10B–12

Remind yourself today, amid your hectic busyness, that God
is with you, that God loves you, that God is protecting you,
and that God is in charge of your life. I like to remind myself,
God is not my copilot; God is my pilot!

1 Samuel 18:6–9; 19:1–7
Psalm 56:2–3,9–10a,10b–11,12–13
Mark 3:7–12

Jesus went up the mountain and summoned those whom he wanted and they came to him.
—MARK 3:13

This is how Mark describes the calling of the twelve apostles. Nothing flowery, nothing exaggerated, just this is what he did, and this is what happened. These men, after the Resurrection, traveled and testified throughout the ancient world. Their testimony was based on their witness of how Jesus had changed their lives. What was the impact of their testimony? Flash forward to today: there are over two billion Christians around the world. The world is permeated with the influence of Jesus and his teachings. In our art, architecture, law, educational systems, hospitals—the list is long. He summoned them, they came, and then they changed everything.

1 Samuel 24:3–21
Psalm 57:2,3–4,6 and 11
Mark 3:13–19

Jesus came with his disciples into the house.
Again the crowd gathered,
making it impossible for them even to eat.
When his relatives heard of this they set out to seize him,
for they said, "He is out of his mind."
—MARK 3:20–21

It's astonishing to realize that several of Jesus' relatives did not recognize his mission and his message. Perhaps that's why Jesus needed to pick twelve strangers to help him. Later in Mark's Gospel, Jesus preaches in his local synagogue. Again, some of those that know him, including relatives, become critical, prompting Jesus to say, "A prophet is not without honor except in his native place and among his own kin and in his own house." Indeed.

2 Samuel 1:1–4,11–12,19,23–27
Psalm 80:2–3,5–7
Mark 3:20–21

Sunday

JANUARY 21

• THIRD SUNDAY IN ORDINARY TIME •

After John had been arrested,
Jesus came to Galilee proclaiming the gospel of God:
"This is the time of fulfillment.
The kingdom of God is at hand.
Repent, and believe in the gospel."
—MARK 1:14–15

Look at the words in this passage:

Fulfillment: provision of what's necessary to deliver on a promise.

Kingdom: the realm in which God's will is fulfilled.

Repent: to turn from sin and dedicate one's life to good.

Believe: to accept as truth.

Gospel: the message of the kingdom, of salvation, of Christ.

Jesus is providing a spiritual roadmap.

Jonah 3:1–5,10
Psalm 25:4–5,6–7,8–9 (4a)
1 Corinthians 7:29–31
Mark 1:14–20

⋗ 50 ⋖

JANUARY 22

• DAY OF PRAYER FOR THE LEGAL PROTECTION OF UNBORN CHILDREN •

And if a house is divided against itself,
that house will not be able to stand.
—MARK 3:25

Many people assume Abraham Lincoln is the author of this
quote, not realizing that Jesus was speaking about
confronting evil in the world. Evil is our undoing; it drives us
against ourselves and one another and brings about our
destruction. Our modern minds don't like to hear about evil
or speak about Satan, but Jesus spoke a great deal about both.
Let's not let the bias of our times prevent us from recognizing
that we are in a constant struggle with forces that do not
wish us well, and however we choose to confront this reality,
let's be clear: denial is not a good strategy.

2 Samuel 5:1–7,10
Psalm 89:20,21–22,25–26
Mark 3:22–30
or, for the Day of Prayer, any readings from the Mass "For Giving Thanks to God for the
Gift of Human Life (*Lectionary for Mass Supplement*, 947A–947E), or the Mass "For Justice and
Peace" (887–891)

JANUARY 23

• ST. VINCENT, DEACON AND MARTYR • ST. MARIANNE COPE, VIRGIN •

> *[Jesus said,] "For whoever does the will of God*
> *is my brother and sister and mother."*
> —MARK 3:35

Yes, Jesus had a family, and he loved his family. But he wants us to know that "whoever does the will of God" is also his family. This should remind us that it's not really Jesus' way to put our family at the center of life.

2 Samuel 6:12b–15,17–19
Psalm 24:7,8,9,10
Mark 3:31–35

JANUARY 24

And when he was alone,
those present along with the Twelve
questioned him about the parables.
—MARK 4:10

Jesus has just shared with a large crowd one of his greatest
teaching stories, the Parable of the Sower. Afterward, his
disciples ask him the meaning of the parable. If you've ever
been puzzled by one of the parables, don't feel bad—you're
in good company. Even those closest to Jesus didn't always
grasp the meaning of his stories. These stories reveal their
meanings in time, when we're ready. They speak to our
hearts as much as to our minds. Our faith makes the soil of
our understanding rich so the wisdom of the parables can
take root and grow within us.

2 Samuel 7:4–17
Psalm 89:4–5,27–28,29–30
Mark 4:1–20

Thursday

JANUARY 25

*"For you will be his witness before all
to what you have seen and heard."*
—ACTS 22:15

Saul, the great persecutor of the early followers of Jesus, after
his famous conversion, becomes Paul, perhaps the greatest of
all the early followers of Jesus. Paul's experience somehow
made clear to him that Jesus had come to be the salvation of
all people. From the moment of his conversion, he worked
tirelessly to bring the Good News to anyone and everyone
who would listen. Fourteen of the twenty-seven books of the
New Testament are attributed to Paul or his influence. He
made five major mission journeys, visited over fifty cities,
and scholars estimate he traveled over ten thousand miles by
foot. Eventually, Paul, like St. Peter, was martyred in Rome.

Acts 22:3–16 or 9:1–22
Psalm 117:1bc,2
Mark 16:15–18

Friday

JANUARY 26

• ST. TIMOTHY AND ST. TITUS, BISHOPS •

For God did not give us a spirit of cowardice
but rather of power and love and self-control.
—2 TIMOTHY 1:7

Focus this day on what is in your control, and surrender to God what is not. There is uncertainty in the world, but there is certainty in God. God will be faithful to you when you are not always faithful. God will be patient with you when you are not always patient. God will be kind to you when you are not always kind. God will be loving to you when you are not always loving. God's faithfulness, patience, kindness, and love rest with God, not with you.

2 Timothy 1:1–8 or Titus 1:1–5
Psalm 96:1–2a,2b–3,7–8a,10
Mark 4:26–34

A clean heart create for me, O God,
and a steadfast spirit renew within me.
—Psalm 51:12

My mother taught me early in life to pray. She wanted me to
know my formal prayers long before my first Holy
Communion, but she also wanted me to know how to speak
informally to God. Learning the Our Father and the Hail
Mary were pretty common practice in Catholic families, but
praying directly to God was not-so-common practice. My
mother also read the Bible—again, not something Catholics
did regularly in the pre-Vatican II 1960s. I remember her
introducing the Psalms to me. She especially loved Psalm 51.
When I hear or read "Create a clean heart in me, O God," I
think of her.

2 Samuel 12:1–7a,10–17
Psalm 51:12–13,14–15,16–17
Mark 4:35–41

JANUARY 28

• FOURTH SUNDAY IN ORDINARY TIME •

Brothers and sisters:
I should like you to be free of anxieties.
—1 CORINTHIANS 7:32

Much is made about Paul's discussion of men and women. In
this passage, he seems to suggest that marriage is a
distraction, with husbands and wives more interested in
pleasing their spouses than pleasing God. This is a
misreading and common misunderstanding of Paul. He
believed deeply that this world was passing soon and that the
kingdom Jesus spoke of was imminent. Paul believed that the
very creation around us was changing, and he didn't want
anyone to be unprepared. He wasn't against marriage; he
simply believed that all our relationships would be different.
For Paul, everything was about Christ's coming.

Deuteronomy 18:15–20
Psalm 95:1–2,6–7,7–9 (8)
1 Corinthians 7:32–35
Mark 1:21–28

JANUARY 29

*But Jesus would not permit him but told him instead,
"Go home to your family and announce to them
all that the Lord in his pity has done for you."*
—MARK 5:19

The story of the Gerasene demoniac, the man who identifies
himself as Legion for the many demons possessing him, is an
important story that appears in the Gospels of Matthew,
Mark, and Luke. Upon being healed, the man wants to go
with Jesus, but Jesus tells him to go back to his family and
tell them what the Lord has done for him. Jesus was very
specific about the people he chose to be with him. But for
many of us, the encounter with Jesus is about going back to
our families and sharing how we've been changed.

2 Samuel 15:13–14,30; 16:5–13
Psalm 3:2–3,4–5,6–7
Mark 5:1–20

Tuesday

JANUARY 30

Disregarding the message that was reported,
Jesus said to the synagogue official,
"Do not be afraid; just have faith."
—MARK 5:36

The phrase "Do not be afraid" appears in some form approximately 365 times in the Bible, depending on which translation we're reading. That's once a day for a year. "Have faith" in some form appears over four hundred times. We should listen to God when he says, "Do not be afraid: just have faith." He means it.

2 Samuel 18:9–10,14b,24–25a,30—19:3
Psalm 86:1–2,3–4,5–6
Mark 5:21–43

JANUARY 31

• ST. JOHN BOSCO, PRIEST •

Then I acknowledged my sin to you;
my guilt I covered not.
I said, "I confess my faults to the LORD,"
and you took away the guilt of my sin.
—PSALM 32:5

I have a journal in which I write prayers. Like the passage above, many seem to address where I've failed and ask the Lord's help and forgiveness:

Forgive me, Lord, the prayers I have not prayed,
the promises I have not kept.
My good intentions unmet with right actions,
the moments of mercy missed by my distracted soul.
Forgive me, Lord,
for failing to share the love
I have so freely been given
and is so undeserved.
Forgive me, Lord, forgive me, Lord.

2 Samuel 24:2,9–17
Psalm 32:1–2,5,6,7
Mark 6:1–6

FEBRUARY 1

When the time of David's death drew near,
he gave these instructions to his son Solomon:
"I am going the way of all flesh.
Take courage and be a man."
—1 KINGS 2:1–2

David's instructions to Solomon are not instructions about being a man but rather about Solomon's having courage to face all that life would bring. For David, that courage was rooted in following the Lord and the promises the Lord had made to David throughout his life. And for David, happiness was found by remaining faithful to God with his whole heart and soul. That's the essential wisdom he wanted to pass on to Solomon before he died.

1 Kings 2:1–4,10–12
1 Chronicles 29:10,11ab,11d–12a,12bcd
Mark 6:7–13

Because he himself was tested through what he suffered,
he is able to help those who are being tested.
—HEBREWS 2:18

As I consider the mystery and suffering of Jesus, I don't get
stuck on his divinity; I get stuck on his humanity. I get stuck
on thinking about all that he suffered, knowing he could
choose not to but accepting and surrendering to the will of
the Father for the redemption and salvation of us all. The
trials and tribulations he suffered, he felt as a human being.
The rejection, the betrayal, the beatings, the scourging, the
nails, the cross—all of it, he felt it just as you and I would.

Malachi 3:1–4
Psalm 24:7,8,9,10
Hebrews 2:14–18
Luke 2:22–40 or 2:22–32

Give your servant, therefore, an understanding heart
to judge your people and to distinguish right from wrong.
—1 KINGS 3:9

Solomon followed his father, David, as king of Israel.
Considered one of the wisest souls who ever lived, his name
is synonymous with making good choices. How did this
come about? Prior to his reign, Solomon sought the advice of
Nathan, one of the greatest prophets of the age. Then he
made a generous sacrifice to the Lord. But perhaps what's
most revealing is the Lord telling Solomon to ask for
anything and it would be given to him. What did Solomon
ask for? He didn't ask for power and wealth but for an
understanding heart to know right from wrong.

1 Kings 3:4–13
Psalm 119:9,10,11,12,13,14
Mark 6:30–34

*Rising very early before dawn, he left
and went off to a deserted place, where he prayed.*
—MARK 1:35

Jesus would often pause during his public ministry and go off
by himself or with a few of his disciples, to pray somewhere
quiet. Why? I believe he sought solitude and quiet for two
reasons: the first was to ask the Father to give him the grace
and courage to do the next right thing and—after that—to
do it again. Then, I imagine Jesus prayed the simplest prayer
of all: "Thank you, Abba."

Job 7:1–4,6–7
Psalm 147:1–2,3–4,5–6
1 Corinthians 9:16–19,22–23
Mark 1:29–39

FEBRUARY 5

• ST. AGATHA, VIRGIN AND MARTYR •

Whatever villages or towns or countryside he entered,
they laid the sick in the marketplaces
and begged him that they might touch only the tassel on his cloak;
and as many as touched it were healed.

—MARK 6:56

In season two, episode three of *The Chosen*, we see Jesus after a long day. He's ministered to and healed countless people. By nightfall, he can barely stand. Only his mother, Mary, has the presence of mind to tend to him as he staggers back into camp, retiring to his tent, exhausted, not having eaten, entirely spent. In that vivid dramatization of the life of Jesus we begin to sense the tremendous, overwhelming need of the crowds clamoring for him, and what it must have cost him.

1 Kings 8:1–7,9–13
Psalm 132:6–7,8–10
Mark 6:53–56

FEBRUARY 6

• ST. PAUL MIKI AND COMPANIONS, MARTYRS •

Look kindly on the prayer and petition of your servant, O LORD,
my God,
and listen to the cry of supplication which I, your servant,
utter before you this day.
—1 KINGS 8:28

We could do worse than begin our days with this beautiful
prayer of Solomon before the altar of the Lord and the
community of Israel. With arms reaching heavenward,
Solomon called on the Lord to hear the prayers of his
people. We hear the echo of Solomon's words in Philippians
4:6, where St. Paul writes, "Have no anxiety at all, but in
everything, by prayer and petition, with thanksgiving, make
your requests known to God." Throughout all of Scripture
this is a dominant theme: God wants to hear our
prayers and petitions.

1 Kings 8:22–23,27–30
Psalm 84:3,4,5 and 10,11
Mark 7:1–13

FEBRUARY 7

*When he got home away from the crowd
his disciples questioned him about the parable.*
—MARK 7:17

Neither the crowds who listen to Jesus, nor those closest to him, the disciples, appear to grasp the meaning of the parables Jesus uses to teach. So why did Jesus use the form of parables to convey important lessons? Parables are a way of cutting through layers and layers of clutter to get to the heart of an insight, almost like a flash of inspiration, but it might take time for it to break through our distracted consciousness. Parables are less concerned about explanation and much more a tool of transformation.

1 Kings 10:1–10
Psalm 37:5–6, 30–31, 39–40
Mark 7:14–23

FEBRUARY 8

• ST. JEROME EMILIANI, PRIEST * ST. JOSEPHINE BAKHITA, VIRGIN •

When Solomon was old his wives had turned his heart to strange gods,
and his heart was not entirely with the LORD, his God.
—1 KINGS 11:4

Though much of Solomon's life is shrouded in myth and
mystery, it proves a great cautionary tale. He starts his reign
by doing everything right, and when the Lord grants him
whatever he wishes, Solomon asks for an understanding heart
to know right from wrong. But alas, as an old man, he turns
from the Lord. Maybe Jesus is thinking of Solomon when he
says, "What profit is there for one to gain the whole world
and forfeit his life?" Solomon not only loses his way toward
the end, but he also loses himself, and in so doing,
loses everything.

1 Kings 11:4–13
Psalm 106:3–4,35–36,37 and 40
Mark 7:24–30

FEBRUARY 9

He ordered them not to tell anyone.
But the more he ordered them not to,
the more they proclaimed it.
—MARK 7:36

Confession is good for the soul, so I want to admit straight up: if I had been with Jesus when he began performing his extraordinary healings and miracles, even though he told me not to say anything, I would probably have told everyone I met what I was witnessing. Surely this was true for the disciples because what they were witnessing was God, active in the world, and how could you not want to share this?! I'm guessing Jesus understood.

1 Kings 11:29–32; 12:19
Psalm 81:10–11ab,12–13,14–15
Mark 7:31–37

FEBRUARY 10

• ST. SCHOLASTICA, VIRGIN •

"My heart is moved with pity for the crowd."
—MARK 8:2

Our church owes much to the early leadership of its great
women, like St. Scholastica. She was the twin sister of St.
Benedict of Nursia, who in the sixth century founded the
Benedictine order. St. Scholastica formed the Benedictine
Sisters based on her brother's Rule. Sadly, not much is known
about her. Here's a brief passage from the Web site of the
Benedictine Sisters of Erie: "She is celebrated by Benedictine
women's religious communities around the world as a woman
who could 'do more because she loved more'" (Gregory the
Great). She was a witness to the truth that love "bears all
things, believes all things, hopes all things, endures all
things. Love never fails" (1 Corinthians 13:7–8).

1 Kings 12:26–32; 13:33–34
Psalm 106:6–7ab,19–20,21–22
Mark 8:1–10

FEBRUARY 11

• SIXTH SUNDAY IN ORDINARY TIME •

Whatever you do,
do everything for the glory of God.
—1 CORINTHIANS 10:31

Each day, our challenge is to intentionally bridge the distance between our creator, God, and ourselves, the created. We can do this in many ways: Through our participation in the sacramental life of the church. Through fellowship with other believers in communal worship. Through stillness and the quiet grace of private prayer. Through devotion to living a virtuous life. Through the simple acts of kindness that come from a willing and loving heart. But most of all, we do this through offering everything to the One who has given us everything. So, whatever we do, as St. Paul encourages us, let's do it all for the glory of God.

Leviticus 13:1–2,44–46
Psalm 32:1–2,5,11 (7)
1 Corinthians 10:31—11:1
Mark 1:40–45

The Pharisees came forward and began to argue with Jesus,
seeking from him a sign from heaven to test him.
He sighed from the depth of his spirit and said,
"Why does this generation seek a sign?"
—MARK 8:11–12

We find a revealing and telling detail about our Lord in this
passage. Jesus had been teaching, healing, and performing
miracles all over the countryside. Word had reached the
Pharisees, and they came to him, wanting him to perform a
sign for them. Now a sign is defined as a quality or event
whose presence or occurrence indicates the probable
presence or occurrence of something else. The first thing
that comes to my mind as I read this: God's standing right in
front of you, but you need a sign?
No wonder Jesus sighed deeply.

James 1:1–11
Psalm 119:67,68,71,72,75,76
Mark 8:11–13

FEBRUARY 13

He said to them, "Do you still not understand?"
—MARK 8:21

Jesus has left the Pharisees who had wanted him to perform a sign. He refused. Now, on a boat, he overhears the disciples worrying about not having brought enough food for their journey. I picture Jesus sighing deeply again and then asking them whether they recall being with him when he fed the multitudes and they ended up with more loaves and fish than they had begun with. When I consider the disciples and their apparent lack of understanding of who Jesus is and how he provides for us, which they have witnessed up close and in spectacular fashion, I'm surprised. But then I stop and recall the extraordinary blessings and gifts I've received from the Lord, and I have to ask myself, "Do I understand?"

James 1:12–18
Psalm 94:12–13a,14–15,18–19
Mark 8:14–21

FEBRUARY 14

• ASH WEDNESDAY •

Even now, says the LORD,
return to me with your whole heart,
with fasting, and weeping, and mourning.
—JOEL 2:12

Today is Ash Wednesday: we mark our foreheads with the blessed and burned ashes of the palm leaves from last year's Palm Sunday. Interestingly, Ash Wednesday service and the receiving of ashes is not a holy day of obligation; attendance is optional. As you look around and see churches overflowing with the faithful on Ash Wednesday, you might wonder why attendance is so high. I suspect that Ash Wednesday is the day Catholics come out in force and declare themselves as Catholics. The marking of the ashes on our foreheads is the public proclamation of our faith, something we can claim in this way only on Ash Wednesday.

Joel 2:12–18
Psalm 51:3–4,5–6ab,12–13,14 and 17
2 Corinthians 5:20—6:2
Matthew 6:1–6,16–18

Thursday

FEBRUARY 15

• THURSDAY AFTER ASH WEDNESDAY •

Then he said to all,
"If anyone wishes to come after me, he must deny himself
and take up his cross daily and follow me.
For whoever wishes to save his life will lose it,
but whoever loses his life for my sake will save it."
—LUKE 9:23–24

I keep a prayer journal, where I write reflections from my prayers and devotional readings. Once, after reading this passage in Luke, I wrote,

It is only in God that we can lose ourselves,
only to find ourselves.
It is only in God that we can lose our way, only to find
our way.
It is only in God that we can lose our lives,
only to find eternal life.

Deuteronomy 30:15–20
Psalm 1:1–2,3,4 and 6
Luke 9:22–25

Friday

FEBRUARY 16

Have mercy on me, O God, in your goodness;
in the greatness of your compassion wipe out my offense.
Thoroughly wash me from my guilt
and of my sin cleanse me.
—PSALM 51:3–4

Lent is a time of repentance, of calling to mind our sinfulness
and asking the Lord for his healing mercy. Lent is also a time
for us to extend that same healing mercy toward others. We
are not alone in our Lenten walk. Shoulder to shoulder, arm
in arm, we are all moving through the mystery of this holy
season, and it is only together that we come through the
pains of Good Friday to the blessings of Easter Sunday.

Isaiah 58:1–9a
Psalm 51:3–4,5–6ab,18–19
Matthew 9:14–15

FEBRUARY 17

"I have not come to call the righteous to repentance but sinners."
—LUKE 5:32

After Jesus calls Matthew the tax collector to follow him, Matthew arranges a large dinner for Jesus. The gathering is attended by other despised tax collectors and "sinners." The Pharisees get wind of this and challenge Jesus on why he wants to hang out with such lowlifes. Jesus responds with the famous Scripture quote above. But what if, rather than referring to the gathered tax collectors and sinners, Jesus is referring to the Pharisees? I've always assumed he was speaking about his dinner mates, but upon a recent reading, I began to think he may have been directing this at the Pharisees themselves.

Isaiah 58:9b–14
Psalm 86:1–2,3–4,5–6
Luke 5:27–32

Sunday

FEBRUARY 18

• FIRST SUNDAY OF LENT •

[Jesus said,] "This is the time of fulfillment.
The kingdom of God is at hand.
Repent, and believe in the gospel."
—MARK 1:15

This is the first Sunday of Lent. We hear Jesus' words upon
returning from forty days and nights in the wilderness
following his baptism by John in the river Jordan. He offers
three short, declarative sentences to send us on our Lenten
way. One that says now's the time. One that says this is the
place. And one that says, rethink everything you think you
know, and believe the good news I'm bringing.

Genesis 9:8–15
Psalm 25:4–5,6–7,8–9
1 Peter 3:18–22
Mark 1:12–15

FEBRUARY 19

You shall love your neighbor as yourself.
—LEVITICUS 19:18

When, in her late seventies, my mother came to live with me, I promised that I would love her and take care of her. Promises made in good conscience. I didn't expect her to have a heart attack. I didn't expect her having to be in a nursing home afterwards. I didn't expect COVID-19, and I didn't expect Mom to die there. But thank God there were strangers who were angels: nurses and nurse's assistants tending to my mother during the worst of the pandemic, staying by her side when I couldn't. Contacting me daily with updates and crying with me on the phone at the end.
Love your neighbor as yourself.
I have experienced this firsthand.

Leviticus 19:1–2,11–18
Psalm 19:8,9,10,15
Matthew 25:31–46

FEBRUARY 20

*I sought the LORD, and he answered me
and delivered me from all my fears.*
—PSALM 34:5

Behind most of our fears, I believe, is the fear of death, and
behind the fear of death lies the fear of oblivion, the loss of
everything we have and everything that makes us who we
are. This is our primal fear, I think. But beyond that fear there
is a freedom. What we have and who we are, are not as
important as who gave us life. We are God's children, created
in the image and likeness of our Creator. If we can find room
in our fear for God, he will not only banish the fear of the
moment, but he will also free us from the fear for all eternity.
This is why we seek God.

Isaiah 55:10–11
Psalm 34:4–5, 6–7, 16–17, 18–19
Matthew 6:7–15

The word of the LORD came to Jonah a second time.
—JONAH 3:1

Jonah's a fascinating character. God gives him an important mission; Jonah refuses and runs away. He catches a ship, trying to escape, gets thrown overboard, is swallowed by a big fish, and is spit out after three days. Then God gives him a second chance: convince the worst people in the worst city to turn from their wicked ways and embrace the Lord. This would appear to be a job for a great prophet, a true believer, not a reluctant one like Jonah. Jonah grumbles but does it, and succeeds fabulously. With God, even the most reluctant of souls can become the greatest of prophets.

Jonah 3:1–10
Psalm 51:3–4,12–13,18–19
Luke 11:29–32

FEBRUARY 22

• THE CHAIR OF ST. PETER THE APOSTLE •

[Jesus said,] "And so I say to you, you are Peter,
and upon this rock I will build my Church."
—MATTHEW 16:18

Jesus saw in Peter something extraordinary, maybe
something Peter did not see in himself. When Jesus asked the
disciples who people said he was, the disciples answered that
some thought he was John the Baptist, others Elijah, still
others Jeremiah or one of the great prophets. When Jesus
asked the disciples who *they* thought he was, Peter answered
immediately, "You are the Christ, the son of the living God."
In that moment, the church we belong to was born and the
man who would lead its first, faltering steps was chosen. Jesus
recognized something special in Peter, but more important,
Peter recognized Jesus as God.

1 Peter 5:1–4
Psalm 23:1–3a,4,5,6
Matthew 16:13–19

• ST. POLYCARP, BISHOP AND MARTYR •

Out of the depths I cry to you, O LORD;
LORD, hear my voice!
Let your ears be attentive
to my voice in supplication.
—PSALM 130:1–2

When I feel my life spinning out of control, I take a beat,
pause for a moment, and remember I am not in
control—God is. I intentionally turn toward God, ask him
for his mercy, and he gently brings me back to a place of
peace. This is God's grace at work, endlessly abundant and
always available for the asking. Don't look to the world for
what only God can give. God is always listening, God always
responds, and love is his only answer.

Ezekiel 18:21–28
Psalm 130:1–2,3–4,5–7a,7bc–8
Matthew 5:20–26

[Jesus said,] "So be perfect, just as your heavenly Father is perfect."
—MATTHEW 5:48

In Matthew's Gospel, the fifth chapter is taken up with the Sermon on the Mount and the teachings that follow on everything from light and the law to anger and adultery, divorce and revenge. Essentially what Jesus does is upend the established order by asking his followers to always go the extra step: turn the other cheek, give your brother or sister the cloak off your back, settle your arguments quickly and generously, forgive your enemies, always give more than you receive, love, and, especially when it's difficult, love more. And then when he concludes his teaching, he offers this last encouragement: "So be perfect, just as your heavenly Father is perfect." I don't know about you, but I have some work to do!

Deuteronomy 26:16–19
Psalm 119:1–2,4–5,7–8
Matthew 5:43–48

FEBRUARY 25

• SECOND SUNDAY OF LENT •

If God is for us, who can be against us?
—ROMANS 8:31B

I stop for a moment and ponder where the Lord of the Universe, the Creator God, the King of kings is active in my small life. And I wonder, if a God as great as the Creator of all, cares about me—really cares about me—and shows it daily, can I but marvel at the kind of God who is my God?

Genesis 22:1–2,9a,10–13,15–18
Psalm 116:10,15,16–17,18–19
Romans 8:31b–34
Mark 9:2–10

FEBRUARY 26

[Jesus said to his disciples:]
"Be merciful, just as your Father is merciful."
—LUKE 6:36

I believe Jesus is asking us to be merciful not only to others but also to ourselves. So do not let your anxiety overwhelm you. Do not let fear take control of you and cause you to worry about things over which you have no control. You do have control about what you choose to focus on. Focus on what you can fix, and leave the rest to God.

Daniel 9:4b–10
Psalm 79:8,9,11 and 13
Luke 6:36–38

FEBRUARY 27

[Jesus said,] "Whoever exalts himself will be humbled;
but whoever humbles himself will be exalted."
—MATTHEW 23:12

I'm a huge country music fan, and I love Tim McGraw. In
2016 he released the song "Humble and Kind," written by
talented songwriter Lori McKenna. She wrote the song for
her husband and five children. She wanted to capture the
essential lessons of life in a nursery-rhyme-like song. I
encourage you to find it and listen to it. Or look up the lyrics
online and sit with them for a while. Simple advice, good,
down-home advice for living well, but the end of every
statement is "Always stay humble and kind." Nursery rhymes
are good for us grownups, too.

Isaiah 1:10,16–20
Psalm 50:8–9,16bc–17,21 and 23
Matthew 23:1–12

FEBRUARY 28

*[Jesus said,] "Just so, the Son of Man did not come to be served
but to serve
and to give his life as a ransom for many."*
—MATTHEW 20:28

These words of Jesus come as he and his disciples are going
to Jerusalem, where Jesus will be tortured, crucified, and then
raised on the third day. How astonishing this must have been
for the disciples to hear. Then Jesus speaks of ransom,
commonly understood to be a payment made to release a
prisoner. In this case, not just one prisoner but "many." Who
are the many? We are. Jesus is the payment that frees us from
the prison of death and makes possible eternal life with him.
As we make our way through Lent, like the disciples made
their way to Jerusalem, it's good to keep this in mind.

Jeremiah 18:18–20
Psalm 31:5–6,14,15–16
Matthew 20:17–28

FEBRUARY 29

I, the LORD, alone probe the mind
and test the heart,
To reward everyone according to his ways,
according to the merit of his deeds.
—JEREMIAH 17:10

The readings today remind us to pay attention, be helpful, and do the right thing. When I was in college, I met a famous inspirational writer in a bookstore. I was actually there buying copies of his books. Over the years he became a mentor to me. He taught me many things that shaped who I have become, but nothing as powerful as when he told me that the greatest lesson in life is simply to be helpful. At first, I was disappointed. How could something so simple be so important? But with each passing year, I understand just how right he was.

Jeremiah 17:5–10
Psalm 1:1–2,3,4 and 6
Luke 16:19–31

Jesus said to them, "Did you never read in the Scriptures:

The stone that the builders rejected
has become the cornerstone;
by the Lord has this been done,
and it is wonderful in our eyes?
—MATTHEW 21:42

A cornerstone is the stone that serves as a foundation for
what is built upon it. In today's readings, both Joseph in
Genesis and Jesus in the parable of the landowner from
Matthew represent the rejected stones that become the
cornerstones. We don't want to see ourselves as those who
rejected Joseph or Jesus. But as I consider these readings, I
ask myself, *What have I rejected? What have I discarded?* I pray
fervently it's not the stone upon which God wishes to build
my faith.

Genesis 37:3–4,12–13a,17b–28a
Psalm 105:16–17,18–19,20–21
Matthew 21:33–43,45–46

[The father said,] "But now we must celebrate and rejoice, because your brother was dead and has come to life again; he was lost and has been found."
—LUKE 15:32

Over the years, my understanding of the story of the prodigal son has changed. When I was a young man, I was so grateful that the father gave his younger son a second chance. Later, I identified with the older brother. I'm a law-abiding, elder-respecting, hardworking guy, not a profligate idiot who burns through his inheritance. Now, I'm an older man, and I see myself in the father, welcoming his lost son home with love, but still concerned that my older, responsible son might feel put out. I'm all the characters in the parable, and therein lies its timeless wisdom.

Micah 7:14–15,18–20
Psalm 103:1–2,3–4,9–10,11–12
Luke 15:1–3,11–32

Sunday

MARCH 3

• THIRD SUNDAY OF LENT •

*For the foolishness of God is wiser than human wisdom,
and the weakness of God is stronger than human strength.*
—1 CORINTHIANS 1:25

After reading these words of St. Paul, you might ask, "What
does *this* mean?!" I admit that it's confusing, in fact,
purposefully confounding. Paul wants to turn our thoughts
upside-down because God's wisdom and strength are not of
this world and cannot be understood through normal ways of
thinking. To quote from *The Wizard of Oz*, "Never question
the truth of what you fail to understand, for the world is
filled with wonders." And there is no wonder greater than the
love God has for each of us.

Exodus 20:1–17 or 20:1–3, 7–8, 12–17
Psalm 19:8,9,10,11
1 Corinthians 1:22–25
John 2:13–25
These readings may be used instead: Ex 17:3–7/Rom 5:1–2, 5–8/Jn 4:5–42 or 4:5–15,
19b–26, 39a, 40–42

Monday

MARCH 4

• ST. CASIMIR •

But he passed through the midst of them and went away.
—LUKE 4:30

Jesus is teaching in the synagogue in Jerusalem. He infuriates
the crowd sufficiently that they try to take him to a hill and
hurl him off. But he passes through them like mist and is
gone. Keep this story in mind when, later in our Lenten
journey, Jesus is turned over to the Romans, where he is
mocked, humiliated, beaten, stripped, scourged, and
crucified. At any point in time, he could have simply faded
into the mist, disappeared, but he didn't. Now ask yourself, if
you had the kind of power Jesus obviously did, could you
have submitted and surrendered to the horrors he faced?

2 Kings 5:1–15ab
Psalm 42:2,3; 43:3,4
Luke 4:24–30

Peter approached Jesus and asked him,
"Lord, if my brother sins against me,
how often must I forgive him?
As many as seven times?"
Jesus answered, "I say to you, not seven times but seventy-seven times."
—MATTHEW 18:21

Jesus encouraged Peter to not ask how many times he needed to forgive but to forgive as often as needed. In 1711, the Enlightenment poet Alexander Pope wrote, "To err is human, to forgive divine." What did Jesus and Pope know about forgiveness? Well, studies show that forgiveness can lead to deeper feelings of understanding, empathy, and compassion; that the act of forgiveness helps lower our risk of heart attack, improves our cholesterol levels, aids in sleep, reduces pain, lowers blood pressure, and helps with anxiety. And that's just in the one doing the forgiving!

Daniel 3:25,34–43
Psalm 25:4–5ab,6 and 7bc,8 and 9
Matthew 18:21–35

*"Do not think that I have come to abolish the law or the prophets.
I have come not to abolish but to fulfill."*
—MATTHEW 5:17

In baseball, late in the game, a relief pitcher called a closer is
sometimes sent in to protect a lead and secure a hard-fought
win. The closer is usually the best relief pitcher and is
capable of striking out batters with blistering speed and
accuracy. The best closers are among the highest paid and
highest impact players in all of major league baseball. They
don't change the game or alter it; they just bring it to a
conclusion for the winning team. I love Matthew 5, verse 17.
When I read it, I think of Jesus as God's closer. Coming into
the game to bring us the win. Glad he's on our side!

Deuteronomy 4:1,5–9
Psalm 147:12–13,15–16,19–20
Matthew 5:17–19

Thursday

MARCH 7

• ST. PERPETUA AND ST. FELICITY, MARTYRS •

Thus says the LORD:
This is what I commanded my people:
Listen to my voice;
then I will be your God and you shall be my people.
—JEREMIAH 7:23

In Frederick Buechner's classic spiritual memoir *Now and Then*
he writes, "Listen to your life." He says listen to it all, even
the tedium and boredom, as well as the joys and triumphs.
Listen during the dead-of-night, can't-sleep times, and listen
during the raging thunderstorms. Listen in the pain, passing
and remaining, and listen in the promises, kept and broken.
Listen to it all, listen to everything, because in the multitude
of cascading moments that make up our lives, God is
speaking to us, always. Listen, for he is our God, and we are
his people.

Jeremiah 7:23–28
Psalm 95:1–2,6–7,8–9
Luke 11:14–23

Friday

MARCH 8

• ST. JOHN OF GOD •

"You shall love the Lord your God with all your heart,
with all your soul,
with all your mind,
and with all your strength.
The second is this:
You shall love your neighbor as yourself.
There is no other commandment greater than these."
—MARK 12:30–31

After a career as a soldier, St. John felt the call of God and opened a house where he tended the sick and the poor for the rest of his days. In a letter he wrote, "For if we share with the poor, out of love for God, whatever He has given to us, we shall receive according to His promise, a hundredfold in eternal happiness." St. John of God lived both great commandments, fully and completely.

Hosea 14:2–10
Psalm 81:6c–8a,8bc–9,10–11ab,14 and 17
Mark 12:28–34

MARCH 9

• ST. FRANCES OF ROME, RELIGIOUS •

For it is love that I desire, not sacrifice,
and knowledge of God rather than burnt offerings.
—HOSEA 6:6

Jesus quotes from Hosea in the Gospel of Matthew, so we
know this is an important Scripture from the Old Testament.
In some versions, *love* is translated as "loyalty," but I find *love*
much more powerful. God wants our love, not our sacrifice.
So, as we make our way through Lent, this is important for us
to reflect upon. God desires our love, and in loving God, we
express the love that first brought us into being. We don't
initiate the love; we simply return it. *That's why God desires our*
love: it is our returning home to him. As the hymn says, "Long have
I waited for your coming home."

Hosea 6:1–6
Psalm 51:3–4,18–19,20–21ab
Luke 18:9–14

Sunday

MARCH 10

• FOURTH SUNDAY OF LENT •

By the streams of Babylon
we sat and wept
when we remembered Zion.
—PSALM 137:1

This powerful psalm of lament evokes the longing for home by the exiled Jews during the Babylonian exile. As we enter the fourth week of Lent, let's reflect on longing for home. Have you ever experienced an inexpressible loss at the core of your being? A bone-deep wanting of something only half-glimpsed in the quiet moments? An ache for a place not quite remembered, but not completely forgotten? A fading dream-vision upon waking that you regret losing in the coming light of day? This is our longing for heaven. Heaven is our home. We will feel this longing until we are reunited with God in that eternity.

2 Chronicles 36:14–16,19–23
Psalm 137:1–2,3,4–5,6 (6ab)
Ephesians 2:4–10
John 3:14–21

Thus says the LORD:
Lo, I am about to create new heavens
and a new earth;
The things of the past shall not be remembered
or come to mind.
—ISAIAH 65:17

God has a "reset" button. When I read Isaiah 65:17, I read it as the Lord's promise to not hold us prisoners of our pasts. The good news is that nothing is permanent. The bad news is that nothing is permanent. So don't let the past cloud your today. Today is a clean slate, a fresh start, a divinely offered do-over. Cherish the opportunity. Begin again. Today we've been given a new heaven and a new earth, and it has been freely offered by a loving God. What will you do with your new day, with your new heaven and earth?

Isaiah 65:17–21
Psalm 30:2 and 4,5–6,11–12a and 13b
John 4:43–54

———————————————

Tuesday

MARCH 12

God is our refuge and our strength,
an ever-present help in distress.
—PSALM 46:2

From my prayer journal . . .

Lord, you are my guide, my protector. Let me not forget
the steadfast hope you have placed in my heart.
Remind me always of your ever-present grace, so
abundantly shared.
Help my awareness to be lit by the light of your presence;
and let my restless heart know the foolishness of my
endless struggling, and to simply have faith and to know
your enduring love.

Ezekiel 47:1–9,12
Psalm 46:2–3,5–6,8–9
John 5:1–16

Wednesday

MARCH 13

*The LORD lifts up all who are falling
and raises up all who are bowed down.*
—PSALM 145:14

Sometimes in prayer, I'm overwhelmed by the suffering I see
in the world. There is an abundance of suffering for which I
seem unable to do anything except pray. But truthfully, what
else can I do? Well, I can look around my world and see who
may be broken, struggling, and carrying their cross. If they
are stumbling, perhaps I can carry their cross for them, even
if just a short distance. I can seek to not add to the suffering
of the world but to bring a measure of mercy instead. I can
try to help, and maybe today, that will be enough.

Isaiah 49:8–15
Psalm 145:8–9,13cd–14,17–18
John 5:17–30

Thursday

MARCH 14

So the LORD relented in the punishment
he had threatened to inflict on his people.
—EXODUS 32:14

Moses implores the Lord to not punish his people for creating a molten calf and worshipping it. The Old Testament is filled with stories like this, where God becomes angry with the Israelites, only to have a great holy man like Moses or one of the prophets plead with him to hold back his punishment and give his people one more chance. We hear that the God of the Old Testament is a harsh God, but often just the opposite appears to be true: the Lord is forever forgiving the transgressions of his people. The Hebrew Scriptures are perhaps better understood as an epic love story between a fickle lover and a faithful God, and, fortunately for us, love always wins.

Exodus 32:7–14
Psalm 106:19–20,21–22,23
John 5:31–47

So they tried to arrest him,
but no one laid a hand upon him,
because his hour had not yet come.
—JOHN 7:30

Things are heating up for Jesus; the authorities want to arrest him. There are plots to kill him. Jesus is cautious where he travels, but his ministry is not complete, so he continues to speak, to teach, and to be highly visible, even though he is in imminent danger. As happens several times in John's Gospel, when Jesus is about to be assaulted, attacked, or arrested, he simply appears to vanish. This passage reminds us that the scheming officials, angry mobs, and violent temple guards are not the ones in charge of this unfolding drama. God is, and nothing will happen, even the death of Jesus, until he ordains it.

Wisdom 2:1a,12–22
Psalm 34:17–18,19–20,21 and 23
John 7:1–2,10,25–30

Some in the crowd who heard these words of Jesus said,
"This is truly the Prophet."
Others said, "This is the Christ."
But others said, "The Christ will not come from Galilee, will he?"
—JOHN 7:40–41

Some who heard Jesus were convinced he was the Messiah, but others who heard him would not believe he could be the Messiah because he came from Galilee. Some of the temple guards were amazed by what they heard from Jesus, but the chief priests and Pharisees discounted their opinions.

Nicodemus argued with his fellow Pharisees, and they dismissed him for not understanding that no great prophet could arise from Galilee. I find it disconcerting that our fixed prejudices and uninformed opinions might allow some of us to miss God standing right in front of us.

Jeremiah 11:18–20
Psalm 7:2–3,9bc–10,11–12
John 7:40–53

In the days when Christ Jesus was in the flesh,
he offered prayers and supplications with loud cries and tears
to the one who was able to save him from death.
—HEBREWS 5:7

Even as the events leading up to Holy Week must have weighed upon Jesus, his faith in the Father was steadfast. No matter what was to come, or how difficult to endure, he trusted in the Father. Our faith is in the same Father Jesus prayed to. The same Father who raised Jesus on the third day into heaven's glorious eternity.

Jeremiah 31:31–34
Psalm 51:3–4,12–13,14–15 (12a)
Hebrews 5:7–9
John 12:20–33

Then Jesus straightened up and said to her,
"Woman, where are they?
Has no one condemned you?"
She replied, "No one, sir."
Then Jesus said, "Neither do I condemn you.
Go, and from now on do not sin any more."
—JOHN 8:10–11

This is the only instance in Scripture when Jesus writes. He writes in the dirt, while kneeling down, while waiting for someone, anyone "who is without sin" to cast the first stone at the woman caught in adultery. Of course, nobody does. But what's important about this story is not what Jesus wrote in the dirt—nobody knows what he wrote; it's his insistence that love is greater than the law. Jesus changes hearts through mercy, not through rules.

Daniel 13:1–9,15–17,19–30,33–62 or 13:41c–62
Psalm 23:1–3a,3b–4,5,6
John 8:1–11

MARCH 19

• ST. JOSEPH, SPOUSE OF THE BLESSED VIRGIN MARY •

When Joseph awoke,
he did as the angel of the Lord had commanded him
and took his wife into his home.
—MATTHEW 1:24

For me, St. Joseph is the patron saint of accountability. I believe that many men, including myself, have accountability issues. Men need to be held accountable to a higher purpose. In the story of St. Joseph, there is no higher purpose than an angel of the Lord coming to you and saying, even though you have not had relations with this woman, yes, she is pregnant, and you will not divorce her. In fact, you will take her into your home, protect her, and raise the child as your own. And Joseph did. That's accountability.

2 Samuel 7:4–5a,12–14a,16
Psalm 89:2–3,4–5,27 and 29
Romans 4:13,16–18,22
Matthew 1:16,18–21,24a or Luke 2:41–51a

Wednesday

MARCH 20

Jesus said to those Jews who believed in him,
"If you remain in my word, you will truly be my disciples,
and you will know the truth, and the truth will set you free."
—JOHN 8:31–32

Jesus is involved in a tense conversation. The people he's
speaking to are like many of us who are defensive about our
beliefs and our identities. Jesus keeps gently suggesting they
might want to listen carefully to exactly what he's saying. But
they won't listen; they continue to argue with him, challenge
him, and finally Jesus says, "Look, if you knew God, then you
would know me; because I came from God. I did not come
on my own, he sent me." This is where most of us might shut
up and pay close attention, rather than keep on arguing
with the Lord.

Daniel 3:14–20,91–92,95
Daniel 3:52,53,54,55,56
John 8:31–42

⇒ 109 ⇐

Look to the LORD in his strength;
seek to serve him constantly.
—PSALM 105:4

Lent is coming to an end, and we are drawing closer to the paschal mysteries, whereby we reflect on the final days of Jesus, his Crucifixion and Resurrection. We consider the themes of sacrifice and redemption. In Holy Thursday, Good Friday, and Easter Sunday we find the roots of our liturgical worship and eucharistic celebration. Also, the symbols that define us: the cross and the empty tomb. The cross is the sign of the ultimate sacrifice of redemptive love. The empty tomb is evidence of our foundational belief: Jesus conquered death, and we who follow him will live with him forever.

Genesis 17:3–9
Psalm 105:4–5,6–7,8–9
John 8:51–59

If I do not perform my Father's works, do not believe me;
but if I perform them, even if you do not believe me,
believe the works, so that you may realize and understand
that the Father is in me and I am in the Father.
—JOHN 10:37–38

Lent is the narrative of Jesus doing the Father's work. And, as the Passion shows, there is nothing easy about the "works" Jesus has undertaken on behalf of the Father. I think of his words in that context, "believe the works." Those works will include the Last Supper, his arrest, and his crucifixion. His last agonizing hours on the cross. Being raised from the dead. Works that not only define our faith but also have quite literally changed the world.

Jeremiah 20:10–13
Psalm 18:2–3a,3bc–4,5–6,7
John 10:31–42

Saturday

MARCH 23

• ST. TORIBIO DE MOGROVEJO, BISHOP •

My dwelling shall be with them;
I will be their God, and they shall be my people.
—EZEKIEL 37:27

The caring love of Yahweh for his people in this passage
from Ezekiel is unmistakably heartfelt. The Lord tells them
he will dwell among them; he will be theirs and they will be
his. This is the covenant expressed as intimately as the
marriage promises between a couple. While the mystery of
God is profound and beyond our comprehension, God's
promise to dwell with us, to be our God and for us to be his
people, is not complicated. It is a proposition of love that
requires a response. Yes, be among us, Lord, and yes, be our
Lord, and yes, we shall be your people. Yes, Lord.

Ezekiel 37:21–28
Jeremiah 31:10,11–12abcd,13
John 11:45–56

Sunday

MARCH 24

• PALM SUNDAY OF THE PASSION OF THE LORD •

Those preceding him as well as those following kept crying out:
"Hosanna!
Blessed is he who comes in the name of the Lord!"
—MARK 11:9

I've always struggled with how the people of Jerusalem could welcome Jesus triumphantly on Palm Sunday, only to turn on him so quickly on Good Friday. Why did this happen? *Hosanna* means "Please, save us!" Perhaps when the people realized Jesus wasn't the kind of king they wanted, their adulation turned to anger. Their "Hosanna" became "Crucify him!" But Jesus did save us, just not in the way people expected. Two thousand years later, do we understand the saving grace Jesus brought, and at what cost?

PROCESSION:
Mark 11:1–10 or John 12:12–16

MASS:
Isaiah 50:4–7
Psalm 22:8–9,17–18,19–20,23–24
Philippians 2:6–11
Mark 14:1—15:47 or 15:1–39

Monday

MARCH 25

• MONDAY OF HOLY WEEK •

Wait for the LORD with courage;
be stouthearted, and wait for the LORD.
—Psalm 27:14

As we enter the last week of Lent and reflect on our journey,
I think there is an important distinction highlighted in the
quote above from Psalm 27. We must wait for the Lord but
wait with courage and be stouthearted, which is another way
of saying be strong and determined. This is not a passive
waiting but an active waiting. Sensing something
momentous. The French philosopher, mystic, and spiritual
writer Simone Weil once wrote, "One does not seek God,
one waits for him." We wait with courage, with strength, and
with the faith that a miraculous turn of events is coming.
Triumph from tragedy. Hope from despair. Light from
darkness. Life from death.

Isaiah 42:1–7
Psalm 27:1,2,3,13–14
John 12:1–11

$\mathscr{T}$uesday
MARCH 26

• TUESDAY OF HOLY WEEK •

Simon Peter said to him, "Master, where are you going?"
Jesus answered him,
"Where I am going, you cannot follow me now,
though you will follow later."
—JOHN 13:36

Judas has now left the Twelve to betray Jesus to the officials looking to arrest him. Jesus has told the apostles he will be with them only a short time, causing them concern and alarm. I believe that what's important in this reading is what Jesus tells Simon Peter. He is leaving them now, and they cannot come with him, but he assures Peter in time, the apostles will understand and follow him once again. Jesus is preparing the way for the apostles, and also for all of us who choose to follow him.

Isaiah 49:1–6
Psalm 71:1–2,3–4a,5ab–6ab,15 and 17
John 13:21–33,36–38

When it was evening,
he reclined at table with the Twelve.
And while they were eating, he said,
"Amen, I say to you, one of you will betray me."
Deeply distressed at this,
they began to say to him one after another,
"Surely it is not I, Lord?"
—MATTHEW 26:20–22

Was Judas truly not aware of who Jesus was? Did his fanaticism override the startling truth of his having been in the presence of God? Was he simply a disillusioned follower hoping for the overthrow of the Romans? In mystery novels, they ask, *"Cui prodest?"* or *"Cui bono?"*—Latin for "Who benefits?" The paradoxical truth is that Judas's betrayal benefited all of us but at the cost of his own life and that of Jesus.

Truly a mystery.

Isaiah 50:4–9a
Psalm 69:8–10,21–22,31 and 33–34
Matthew 26:14–25

Thursday

MARCH 28

• THURSDAY OF HOLY WEEK (HOLY THURSDAY) •

If I, therefore, the master and teacher, have washed your feet,
you ought to wash one another's feet.
I have given you a model to follow,
so that as I have done for you, you should also do.
—JOHN 13:14–15

Much of Scripture can be difficult to understand. But the story of Jesus washing the feet of the apostles in John 13 is not hard to understand. In fact, Jesus spells it out plainly for the apostles. He is the master, and he has washed their feet. This is the model they are to follow. In Christ's kingdom, the mighty serve the lowly.

CHRISM MASS:
Isaiah 61:1–3a,6a,8b–9
Psalm 89:21–22,25,27
Revelation 1:5–8
Luke 4:16–21

EVENING MASS OF THE LORD'S SUPPER:
Exodus 12:1–8,11–14
Psalm 116:12–13,15–16bc,17–18
1 Corinthians 11:23–26
John 13:1–15

Friday

MARCH 29

• FRIDAY OF THE PASSION OF THE LORD (GOOD FRIDAY) •

So Pilate said to him,
"Do you not speak to me?
Do you not know that I have power to release you
and I have power to crucify you?"
Jesus answered him,
"You would have no power over me
if it had not been given to you from above."
—JOHN 19:10–11A

The Greek word for "power" as it is used in the New Testament is *dunamis*, the word from which we get *dynamite*. Jesus did have tremendous power, but his real power was holding that power in check. If Pilate knew the real power Jesus possessed, he might have been terrified. But Pilate didn't recognize the truth, let alone the Lord standing right in front of him.

Isaiah 52:13—53:12
Psalm 31:2,6,12–13,15–16,17,25
Hebrews 4:14–16; 5:7–9
John 18:1—19:42

If, then, we have died with Christ,
we believe that we shall also live with him.
—ROMANS 6:8

St. Paul is summing up two pillars of our Christian belief.
One, we who have died with Christ spiritually will be reborn
and live a new life with Christ spiritually in the here and
now. Two, we who will eventually die physically will be
restored and raised to live with Christ in eternity. This is the
heart of the paschal mystery as we close our Lenten journey.

VIGIL:
Genesis 1:1—2:2 or 1:1,26–31a
Psalm 104:1–2,5–6,10,12,13–14,24,35 or
33:4–5,6–7,12–13,20–22
Genesis 22:1–18 or 22:1–2,9a,10–13,15–18
Psalm 16:5,8,9–10,11
Exodus 14:15—15:1
Exodus 15:1–2,3–4,5–6,17–18
Isaiah 54:5–14
Psalm 30:2,4,5–6,11–12,13
Isaiah 55:1–11

Isaiah 12:2–3,4,5–6
Baruch 3:9–15,32—4:4
Psalm 19:8,9,10,11
Ezekiel 36:16–17a,18–28
Psalm 42:3,5; 43:3,4 or Isaiah
12:2–3,4bcd,5–6 or Psalm
51:12–13,14–15,18–19
Romans 6:3–11
Psalm 118:1–2,16–17,22–23
Mark 16:1–7

Sunday

MARCH 31

• EASTER SUNDAY OF THE RESURRECTION OF THE LORD •

On the first day of the week,
Mary of Magdala came to the tomb early in the morning,
while it was still dark,
and saw the stone removed from the tomb.
—JOHN 20:1

I recently bought a T-shirt that reads "A lot can happen in 3 days." There are three images on the front of the shirt: a crown of thorns, a cross, and an empty tomb. A brilliant, shorthand example of something as commonplace as a T-shirt capturing the immense truth and mystery of the Passion.

Acts 10:34a,37–43
Psalm 118:1–2,16–17,22–23
Colossians 3:1–4 or 1 Corinthians 5:6b–8
John 20:1–9 or Mark 16:1–7 or, at an afternoon or evening Mass, Luke 24:13–35

I bless the LORD who counsels me;
even in the night my heart exhorts me.
—PSALM 16:7

Have you ever woken up at three in the morning and not been able to go back to sleep? Maybe you have something weighing heavily on you? The middle of the night can be a lonely, scary time. In his song "Good Good Father," Chris Tomlin speaks of hearing God's tender whisper in the dead of night, reminding him he is loved and never alone. This is what David is speaking about in the passage above from Psalm 16. God is speaking to us with gentle words of comfort, letting us know we are loved and that he is with us, even in the darkest hours of the long night.

Acts 2:14,22–33
Psalm 16:1–2a and 5,7–8,9–10,11
Matthew 28:8–15

Tuesday

APRIL 2

• TUESDAY WITHIN THE OCTAVE OF EASTER •

When she had said this, she turned around and saw Jesus there,
but did not know it was Jesus.

—JOHN 20:14

There are ten post-Resurrection appearances of Jesus
recorded in the Bible. John writes in the last passage of his
Gospel, "There are also many other things that Jesus did, but
if these were to be described individually, I do not think the
whole world would contain the books that would be written"
(John 21:25). What's interesting to me about the first
post-Resurrection appearances is that Jesus' followers don't
appear to recognize him. Perhaps the human Jesus disciples
had known was now the risen Christ. The same, and yet
different, transformed.

Acts 2:36–41
Psalm 33:4–5,18–19,20 and 22
John 20:11–18

Wednesday

APRIL 3

• WEDNESDAY WITHIN THE OCTAVE OF EASTER •

Peter said, "I have neither silver nor gold,
but what I do have I give you:
in the name of Jesus Christ the Nazorean, rise and walk."
—ACTS 3:6

John and Peter are walking to prayer when they see a man
begging outside the temple. Peter says, "Look at us." He tells
the man they have no gold or silver for him, only Jesus. Then
Peter offers him his hand, raises him up, and the man is
healed. As they walk into the temple together, the man is
"jumping and praising God." And though Scripture doesn't
mention it, I'm certain John and Peter were rejoicing too.

Acts 3:1–10
Psalm 105:1–2,3–4,6–7,8–9
Luke 24:13–35

Thursday

APRIL 4

• THURSDAY WITHIN THE OCTAVE OF EASTER •

While they were still speaking about this,
he stood in their midst and said to them,
"Peace be with you."
But they were startled and terrified
and thought that they were seeing a ghost.
—LUKE 24:36–37

The two disciples recount meeting Jesus on the way to Emmaus but not recognizing him until the breaking of the bread. As they finish telling their story, Jesus suddenly appears to all the disciples gathered. There's much in these post-Resurrection stories to reflect on, but one theme that stands out for me is that God meets us where we are. God always crosses the bridge from the divine to the human. We simply need to have eyes that see and minds that are open.

Acts 3:11–26
Psalm 8:2ab and 5,6–7,8–9
Luke 24:35–48

Friday

APRIL 5

• FRIDAY WITHIN THE OCTAVE OF EASTER •

*When it was already dawn, Jesus was standing on the shore;
but the disciples did not realize that it was Jesus.*
—JOHN 21:4

Early in Luke's Gospel, after a long night of unsuccessful
fishing, Peter meets Jesus for the first time. Jesus urges him to
cast his nets one more time. Peter agrees, and the catch is so
large it almost capsizes the boat. In John's Gospel,
post-Resurrection, after another night of unsuccessful fishing,
Peter spots the risen Jesus on the shore. Jesus urges Peter to
cast his nets again, and the catch nearly capsizes their boat.
In each story, however weary and tired Peter might be, Peter
says yes to Jesus. And each time, the result is a miracle.

Acts 4:1–12
Psalm 118:1–2 and 4,22–24,25–27a
John 21:1–14

*I will give thanks to you, for you have answered me
and have been my savior.*
—PSALM 118:21

At a difficult time, I called a good friend, a man of great faith,
who knew of my life's circumstances. He listened, was
supportive and kind. I told him how bad I was feeling that
particular day. He reminded me that God was closest to me
while I was at my lowest. He encouraged me to pray, to ask
God for help, but also to listen and pay close attention to
what I heard and felt. I did as he suggested, and in time, I felt
the gentle, loving presence of God. God is always with us,
waiting; we simply need to stop and let his gentle peace in.

Acts 4:13–21
Psalm 118:1 and 14–15ab,16–18,19–21
Mark 16:9–15

Sunday

APRIL 7

• SECOND SUNDAY OF EASTER (OR SUNDAY OF DIVINE MERCY) •

Then [Jesus] said to Thomas,
"Put your finger here and see my hands,
and bring your hand and put it into my side,
and do not be unbelieving, but believe."
—JOHN 20:27

It's easy to be a little smug when we hear the story of Thomas needing to see the wounds of Jesus before believing he is the risen Lord. But perhaps Thomas was a pragmatist, and this appealed to Jesus and may explain why he chose him to be a disciple. Thomas needed facts rather than accepting something on blind faith. We all have a little doubting Thomas in us, and Jesus knows this. So, maybe it's not only to Thomas that Jesus is saying, "Do not be unbelieving, but believe."

Acts 4:32–35
Psalm 118:2–4,13–15,22–24
1 John 5:1–6
John 20:19–31

Mary said, "Behold, I am the handmaid of the Lord.
May it be done to me according to your word."
Then the angel departed from her.
—LUKE 1:38

The Annunciation not only celebrates the incarnation of
Jesus to Mary (and the world) but also the coming birth of
John to Mary's cousin Elizabeth. An angel does the
announcing, and not just any angel but Gabriel, the
archangel who appeared to Daniel in the Hebrew Bible to
explain the prophet's visions. Gabriel tells Mary she is
pregnant by a miracle of the Holy Spirit. Gabriel tells Mary
not to worry, then departs. While processing all this
incredible news, alone and maybe sixteen years old, Mary
says to the Lord, "May it be done to me according to
your word."

Isaiah 7:10–14; 8:10
Psalm 40:7–8a,8b–9,10,11
Hebrews 10:4–10
Luke 1:26–38

*[Jesus said,] "The wind blows where it wills, and you can hear
the sound it makes,
but you do not know where it comes from
or where it goes."*
—JOHN 3:8

Nicodemus is a man of great learning, respected among his
priestly class. By the world's measure, an expert on God. Jesus
is meeting quietly, secretly, with Nicodemus. When Jesus
seeks to explain the workings of his Father, he basically tells
Nicodemus that God cannot be known. That God is like the
wind: you can feel it, you can hear it, but you don't know
where it comes from or where it will go. How must this have
sounded to Nicodemus, a devout man who spent his life
trying to know God, only to be told, by God, that no man
can know God?

Acts 4:32–37
Psalm 93:1ab,1cd–2,5
John 3:7b–15

*God so loved the world that he gave his only-begotten Son,
so that everyone who believes in him might not perish
but might have eternal life.*
—JOHN 3:16

In John 3:16, all of Scripture appears to be simplified into an
elegant statement of belief. God gave us Jesus, and all who
believe in Jesus will never die.

Acts 5:17–26
Psalm 34:2–3,4–5,6–7,8–9
John 3:16–21

Thursday

APRIL 11

The LORD is close to the brokenhearted;
and those who are crushed in spirit he saves.
—PSALM 34:19

We all have bad days. I had a bad year—so bad in fact, getting out of bed was a challenge. If something could go wrong, it did. While things could have been worse, I don't think they could have been much worse. But what I learned was exactly what the psalmist speaks of: the Lord was close, and each day that I walked in the valley of the shadow of death, I knew he was with me. To this day, I can attest that the Lord was closest to me when I needed him most.

Acts 5:27–33
Psalm 34:2 and 9,17–18,19–20
John 3:31–36

One thing I ask of the LORD;
this I seek:
To dwell in the house of the LORD
all the days of my life.
—PSALM 27:4

I was a military brat; my father was in the Air Force. We followed planes around the world, whichever one my father was working on at the time. My mother once wrote down for me the twenty-six different addresses I lived at before I was sixteen. Then there were another couple of dozen after that. We were modern nomads with no real home. Psalm 27 speaks to my heart and my desire to find a home. As I've grown in my faith and come to know the Lord, I can't think of a more perfect prayer for this wanderer than "Please Lord, let me dwell with you all the rest of my days."

Acts 5:34–42
Psalm 27:1,4,13–14
John 6:1–15

APRIL 13

• ST. MARTIN I, POPE AND MARTYR •

When they had rowed about three or four miles,
they saw Jesus walking on the sea and coming near the boat,
and they began to be afraid.
But he said to them, "It is I. Do not be afraid."
—JOHN 6:19–20

Jesus walking on the water takes place three times in the Gospels, so we know it's significant. But is the significance Jesus walking on the water? Or could it be that the disciples, far from shore, late at night, in a storm, see Jesus but don't recognize him? Jesus tells them it's him and not to be afraid. They do recognize him then, and miraculously they arrive safely at their intended destination. Perhaps the miracle is recognizing that Jesus is always with us, no matter where, no matter what, bringing us safely through the storm.

Acts 6:1–7
Psalm 33:1–2,4–5,18–19
John 6:16–21

Sunday

APRIL 14

• THIRD SUNDAY OF EASTER •

Then he said to them, "Why are you troubled?
And why do questions arise in your hearts?"
—LUKE 24:38

Sometimes, when I read a question like this from Jesus, I take it very personally. Why am I troubled? Why do questions arise in my heart? Is it the recognition of how broken things can appear at times? While we can recognize the world's brokenness, God's love asks us to respond with a willed choice to love fiercely anyway. This is what Jesus was so often inviting us to do. When we're troubled and have heavy hearts, we fail to see that God's love can heal the broken parts of our lives, and the world, into wholeness. Jesus is asking the questions, to which he is the answer.

Acts 3:13–15,17–19
Psalm 4:2,4,7–8,9 (7a)
1 John 2:1–5a
Luke 24:35–48

So they said to him,
"What can we do to accomplish the works of God?"
Jesus answered and said to them,
"This is the work of God, that you believe in the one he sent."
—JOHN 6:28–29

This exchange takes place after the feeding of the five thousand. The crowds are clamoring for Jesus, wanting to know more about him, who he is, where he's from, anything to understand this mysterious, miracle-working wonder. Jesus tells them, "Believe in me and you are doing the work of God." While this exchange happened two thousand years ago, the proposition remains the same. When we ask what God wants of us, the answer is still, "Believe in the one I sent."

Acts 6:8–15
Psalm 119:23–24,26–27,29–30
John 6:22–29

APRIL 16

Let your face shine upon your servant;
save me in your kindness.
—PSALM 31:17

No matter how cruel and violent the world may appear, I believe God is always with us. In countless stories of selfless martyrs, like the stoning of Stephen in today's reading from Acts, we see in moments of sheer terror the martyrs appearing calm, almost serene before they die. Luke writes that Stephen was filled with the Holy Spirit and saw a vision of heaven with Jesus standing at the right side of God, and as he is dying, like Jesus, Stephen asks forgiveness for his killers. What's going on here? How can something so terrifying be met with such equanimity? I believe it is the saving grace of God.

Acts 7:51—8:1a
Psalm 31:3cd–4,6 and 7b and 8a,17 and 21ab
John 6:30–35

Wednesday

APRIL 17

Jesus said to the crowds,
"I am the bread of life;
whoever comes to me will never hunger,
and whoever believes in me will never thirst."
—JOHN 6:35

I don't believe Jesus is using an analogy here. It is by following him faithfully and believing in him absolutely that we will be fed, nourished, and sustained. Not simply to feed and sustain the hunger of the body, or the mind, or the heart, but our very existence. By believing in Jesus, we are given meaning, purpose, and sustenance. This is not symbolic language, or theology, or ideology. This is the foundational truth of our faith: believing in Jesus gives us life.

Acts 8:1b–8
Psalm 66:1–3a,4–5,6–7a
John 6:35–40

When I appealed to him in words,
praise was on the tip of my tongue.
—PSALM 66:17

All prayer is essentially praise and thanksgiving. When we
petition the Lord, let it be from hearts full of gratitude.
Before we ask God for something, let us first thank him for
what he has already given us.

Acts 8:26–40
Psalm 66:8–9,16–17,20
John 6:44–51

Friday

APRIL 19

*On his journey, as he was nearing Damascus,
a light from the sky suddenly flashed around him.
He fell to the ground and heard a voice saying to him,
"Saul, Saul, why are you persecuting me?"
He said, "Who are you, sir?"
The reply came, "I am Jesus, whom you are persecuting."*
—ACTS 9:3–5

The conversion of St. Paul is a remarkable story. Paul moved Jesus beyond the Jewish faith and into the mainstream of his time. If Paul had not come on the scene and done what he did, Christianity would likely be an obscure branch of Judaism that never made it out of Palestine. But Paul convinced Peter and the other disciples to see that Jesus was the Messiah for *all* people. Paul pushed the faith into the very heart of Rome and forever changed history.

Acts 9:1–20
Psalm 117:1bc,2
John 6:52–59

Jesus then said to the Twelve, "Do you also want to leave?"
Simon Peter answered him, "Master, to whom shall we go?
You have the words of eternal life.
We have come to believe
and are convinced that you are the Holy One of God."
—JOHN 6:67–69

God bless St. Peter! When other disciples and followers were beginning to drop off, Jesus asks the Twelve if they also want to leave. It's Peter who speaks up, as he often does. No Lord, where would we go now and how could we possibly live without you, knowing who you really are? There's a reason Jesus chose Peter to be the foundation stone of the church. It was because Peter, despite all of his human failings and faults, repeatedly chose Jesus. Peter's faith was fierce.

Acts 9:31–42
Psalm 116:12–13,14–15,16–17
John 6:60–69

APRIL 21

• FOURTH SUNDAY OF EASTER •

Beloved, we are God's children now;
what we shall be has not yet been revealed.
We do know that when it is revealed we shall be like him,
for we shall see him as he is.
—1 JOHN 3:2

When I was a boy, I worried about living on my own, having
my own home. I worried especially about how to operate the
thermostat. How could I heat and cool my house if I didn't
know how to do this one simple task? My father reassured
me that he would show me what I would need to know,
including how to operate a thermostat, and he did. The Lord
is like a good parent: he will reveal what we need to know
when we need to know it.

Acts 4:8–12
Psalm 118:1,8–9,21–23,26,28,29 (22)
1 John 3:1–2
John 10:11–18

And bring me to your holy mountain,
to your dwelling-place.
—PSALM 43:3B

As a military brat, I've often thought about what home means, or as Scripture might say it, a dwelling place. At Mass the other evening, the priest told the story of a traveler visiting a large city in a foreign country, home to a renowned spiritual teacher. The traveler went to see the teacher. Knocking on his door, he was welcomed into a spartan, one-room apartment, furnished with a bed, a table and chair, and some well-stocked bookshelves. The traveler asked, "Teacher, where is your furniture?"

The teacher asked, "Where is yours?"
"But I'm only passing through, just a visitor here."
"So am I," said the teacher.

Acts 11:1–18
Psalm 42:2–3; 43:3–4
John 10:1–10

Tuesday

APRIL 23

• ST. GEORGE, MARTYR • ST. ADALBERT, BISHOP AND MARTYR •

So the Jews gathered around him and said to him,
"How long are you going to keep us in suspense?
If you are the Christ, tell us plainly."
—JOHN 10:24

I'm puzzled by the people who actually saw Jesus but did not recognize him. I pray I would not have been one of them. Mark Nepo, in *The Book of Awakening*, writes, "If you can't see what you're looking for, see what's there." These people were looking for the Messiah, and he was standing there in plain sight, teaching, healing, and performing miracles. Not only did they not see what they were looking for, they did not see what was right there.

Acts 11:19–26
Psalm 87:1b–3,4–5,6–7
John 10:22–30

⇒ 143 ⇐

APRIL 24

• ST. FIDELIS OF SIGMARINGEN, PRIEST AND MARTYR •

I came into the world as light,
so that everyone who believes in me might not remain in darkness.
—JOHN 12:46

St. Fidelis was a lawyer who became a Capuchin monk during the Counter-Reformation. He died a terrible death for standing up to a violent anti-Catholic mob. But firsthand accounts suggest that, like many martyrs, he was fearless. He was canonized in 1746, more than a century after his death. During his canonization process, more than three hundred miracles were attributed to his intercession. St. Fidelis is quoted as saying, "It is because of faith that we exchange the present for the future."

Acts 12:24—13:5a
Psalm 67:2–3,5,6 and 8
John 12:44–50

Thursday

APRIL 25

• ST. MARK, EVANGELIST •

Jesus appeared to the Eleven and said to them:
"Go into the whole world
and proclaim the Gospel to every creature."
—MARK 16:15

This commission to proclaim the gospel to every creature perhaps had its greatest adherent in St. Francis of Assisi, who, like the apostles, changed the world with his preaching and teaching. One of the stories that has survived the ages is Francis preaching to the birds. "My sweet little sisters, birds of the sky, you are bound to heaven, to God, your Creator. In every beat of your wings and every note of your songs, praise him." According to eyewitnesses, the birds listened politely to Francis while he preached to them. Francis took Jesus at his word and preached the gospel to "every creature."

1 Peter 5:5b–14
Psalm 89:2–3,6–7,16–17
Mark 16:15–20

Friday

APRIL 26

*Jesus said to him, "I am the way and the truth and the life.
No one comes to the Father except through me."*
—JOHN 14:6

Jesus is addressing this famous quote to Thomas—yes, that
Thomas—while trying to explain to the apostles where he
will be going soon and how they will follow him. Thomas is
looking for directions as a person would ask for a map. But
this isn't what Jesus is talking about. Jesus *is* the departure
point, the journey, and the destination. Not an easy concept
to grasp. This is not a trip we embark upon by using GPS.
Jesus is telling Thomas, and the other apostles, that they will
know the way because they know Jesus and have faith in
him. This is the truth for us as well.

Acts 13:26–33
Psalm 2:6–7,8–9,10–11ab
John 14:1–6

⇒ 146 ⇐

Saturday

APRIL 27

[Jesus said,] "If you ask anything of me in my name, I will do it."
—JOHN 14:14

I'm a serious pray-er and have an elaborate morning ritual
that involves breathing, an invocation, lighting a candle, and
reading from an old Catholic prayer book that most of the
pages have fallen out of. One of the aspects of my morning
prayer is to read the promises of Jesus, which I have copied
out of Scripture and printed out. I read these promises of
Jesus because they are astounding and I don't want to ever
forget them. Like the one above, John 14:14: "If you ask
anything of me in my name, I will do it." I find this promise
so amazing that I always begin my prayer time with a heart
full of gratitude.

Acts 13:44–52
Psalm 98:1,2–3ab,3cd–4
John 14:7–14

*[Jesus said,] "If you remain in me and my words remain in you,
ask for whatever you want and it will be done for you."*
—JOHN 15:7

Another incredible promise of Jesus. Teresa of Ávila said,
"You find God in yourself and yourself in God." Each day we
give ourselves to God, and each day, God gives himself to us.
It is in that glorious exchange that we are transformed, loved,
and redeemed.

Acts 9:26–31
Psalm 22:26–27,28,30,31–32 (26a)
1 John 3:18–24
John 15:1–8

[Jesus said,] "I have told you this while I am with you.
The Advocate, the Holy Spirit
whom the Father will send in my name—
he will teach you everything
and remind you of all that I told you."
—JOHN 14:25–26

Today we celebrate one of our greatest saints and a doctor of
the church. Catherine lived a short life, dying at thirty-three,
but was hugely influential in her time (1347–1380). She was
a third order Dominican and attended to the sick and the
poor. Her severe fasting probably caused her premature
death. Before she died, she wrote a major work called *The
Dialogue*, which is still in print more than five hundred
years later.

Acts 14:5–18
Psalm 115:1–2,3–4,15–16
John 14:21–26

Tuesday

APRIL 30

• ST. PIUS V, POPE •

Jesus said to his disciples:
"Peace I leave with you; my peace I give to you.
Not as the world gives do I give it to you.
Do not let your hearts be troubled or afraid."
—JOHN 14:27

Jesus offers us peace, but not the peace of this world. It is a peace freely given. It is a peace that endures. It is a peace that frees our troubled hearts and our restless, fearful minds. It is a peace born of heaven and carried into the world by the Holy Spirit. It is a peace first offered to the apostles two thousand years ago by Jesus. It is a peace still being offered to each of us two thousand years later by that same Holy Spirit.

Acts 14:19–28
Psalm 145:10–11,12–13ab,21
John 14:27–31a

⇒ 150 ⇐

Wednesday
MAY 1

• ST. JOSEPH THE WORKER •

[Jesus said,] "If you remain in me and my words remain in you,
ask for whatever you want and it will be done for you."
—JOHN 15:7

Today the church celebrates one of the two feasts of St.
Joseph. Begun in 1955 by Pope Pius XII, this day honors
workers worldwide. My father's name was Joseph. I was
named after him and, coincidently, born in 1955. St. Joseph
has always been a steadfast model of virtue and responsibility
for me. As a man, you take care of your family. You watch
over and protect your wife and children. You provide for
them by working hard. St. Joseph was accountable,
dependable, and hardworking. I'm honored to have been
named for both my father and St. Joseph.

Acts 15:1–6
Psalm 122:1–2,3–4ab,4cd–5
John 15:1–8 or Matthew 13:54–58

Sing to the LORD a new song;
sing to the LORD, all you lands.
—PSALM 96:1

Reason #23 for Going to Church

I can't sing; in fact, I can't carry a note to save my soul. My lack of vocal skill means I usually sing only in the shower or when I'm driving, alone. But there is one place I do get to sing, and that's in church. If I don't sing too loud, I can blend my voice with the choir and the congregation and sing a beautiful song like Dan Schutte's "Here I Am, Lord." So, if you're like me and don't sing well but still love to sing, go to church. All are welcome, trust me, even the tone deaf.

Acts 15:7–21
Psalm 96:1–2a,2b–3,10
John 15:9–11

MAY 3

• ST. PHILIP AND ST. JAMES, APOSTLES •

"Amen, amen, I say to you,
whoever believes in me will do the works that I do,
and will do greater ones than these,
because I am going to the Father.
And whatever you ask in my name, I will do,
so that the Father may be glorified in the Son.
If you ask anything of me in my name, I will do it."
—JOHN 14:12–14

I find this passage from John remarkable. I recommend you commit this passage to memory or write it down so you won't lose track of it. Anytime you're feeling down, worried, or anxious, I urge you to find a quiet moment and read this passage slowly to yourself and believe it.

1 Corinthians 15:1–8
Psalm 19:2–3,4–5
John 14:6–14

Saturday

MAY 4

The LORD is good:
his kindness endures forever,
and his faithfulness, to all generations.
—PSALM 100:5

This is a purely unscientific claim, but in my experience, over a lifetime, I've found that not only is the Lord good and kind but so are most people. Being good, being kind creates a ripple effect in the world. Don't overthink what life is asking of you; sometimes it's enough to be good and kind. Often, it's more than enough.

Acts 16:1–10
Psalm 100:1b–2,3,5
John 15:18–21

Sunday

MAY 5

• SIXTH SUNDAY OF EASTER •

Then Peter proceeded to speak and said,
"In truth, I see that God shows no partiality."
—ACTS 10:34

Coming toward the end of the section in Matthew's Gospel that features the Sermon on the Mount, Jesus says this: "But I say to you, love your enemies, and pray for those who persecute you, that you may be children of your heavenly Father, *for he makes his sun rise on the bad and the good, and causes rain to fall on the just and the unjust."* The italics are mine. Jesus, and Peter in the passage above, are stating a profound truth: God doesn't love us more because we're good; God loves all of us equally because God is good.

Acts 10:25–26,34–35,44–48
Psalm 98:1,2–3,3–4 (see 2b)
1 John 4:7–10
John 15:9–17

⇒ 155 ⇐

Monday

MAY 6

One of them, a woman named Lydia, a dealer in purple cloth,
from the city of Thyatira, a worshiper of God, listened,
and the Lord opened her heart to pay attention
to what Paul was saying.
—ACTS 16:14

People sometimes assume that Paul didn't like women, but this is patently wrong. While researching a small book about St. Paul, I discovered that many women were instrumental in his ministry. Paul would often preach and teach in the homes of prominent women. These homes were called "house churches." In time, some of these same women became influential leaders within the growing Christian movement. Not only were women the first to witness the resurrected Lord, but they were also among the first to organize early communities of Christian worship.

Acts 16:11–15
Psalm 149:1b–2,3–4,5–6a and 9b
John 15:26—16:4a

When I called, you answered me;
you built up strength within me.
—PSALM 138:3

Prayer is the act of calling upon God, and we do this as the
persistent, unapologetic, flawed, imperfect, incomplete soul
that each of us is. Prayer is most powerful when we call upon
God—but also when we listen to God. The only people who
are good at prayer are those who keep trying to pray.

Acts 16:22–34
Psalm 138:1–2ab,2cde–3,7c–8
John 16:5–11

Wednesday

MAY 8

Jesus said to his disciples:
"I have much more to tell you, but you cannot bear it now."
—JOHN 16:12

Jesus knew that the disciples would need to live into the truth of what was to come once he was gone. He couldn't prepare them for everything they would face. He promised them an advocate, the Holy Spirit, and he gave them certain powers in his name and in his Father's name. But ultimately, the disciples would need to make good choices, discern their paths, and live in the same faith we're called to live in today.

Acts 17:15,22—18:1
Psalm 148:1–2,11–12,13,14
John 16:12–15

Thursday

MAY 9

• THE ASCENSION OF THE LORD •

*So then the Lord Jesus, after he spoke to them,
was taken up into heaven
and took his seat at the right hand of God.*
—MARK 16:19

Imagine the disciples spending three years with this amazing teacher Jesus, coming to believe he was the Son of God, the Messiah. They see him work astonishing miracles and life-altering healings. They witness his crucifixion, death, and burial. Then he reappears and walks among them for another forty days. Until one day, he walks all of them to a field in the countryside, leaves his final instructions, and then rises heavenward, taking his rightful place beside God. Talk about a Hollywood ending!

Acts 1:1–11
Psalm 47:2–3,6–7,8–9 (6)
Ephesians 1:17–23 or 4:1–13 or 4:1–7,11–13
Mark 16:15–20
*In Provinces where the celebration of Ascension is transferred to the Seventh Sunday of Easter, the following
readings are used on this Thursday: Acts 18:1–8/Jn 16:16–20*

Friday

MAY 10

• ST. DAMIEN DE VEUSTER, PRIEST •

One night while Paul was in Corinth, the Lord said to him in a vision,
"Do not be afraid.
Go on speaking, and do not be silent, for I am with you."
—ACTS 18:9–10A

Paul was almost always on the road. His ministry took him all over the ancient world. For God to tell Paul to stay put for a while was significant, and to stay put in Corinth, the Sin City of the Greek world, was even more interesting. But Paul did stay, almost two years, and while there he wrote one of the most memorable pieces of literature on love in the entire Western canon: the thirteenth chapter of 1 Corinthians. *"Love is patient, love is kind. It does not envy, it does not boast, it is not proud"* (emphasis added).

Acts 18:9–18
Psalm 47:2–3,4–5,6–7
John 16:20–23

Saturday

MAY 11

*[Jesus said,] "Until now you have not asked anything in my name;
ask and you will receive, so that your joy may be complete."*
—JOHN 16:24

There is nothing ambiguous, confusing, obtuse, or unclear
about what Jesus tells the disciples in this passage. It's
another startling promise of Jesus. He's preparing to leave the
disciples and is offering them his last thoughts, his final
instructions. Jesus is not bound by time or space, so what he
promises the disciples of two thousand years ago remains as
valid for us—the disciples of today—as it was then. This
jaw-dropping promise by Jesus states that anything we ask in
his name will be given to us. And why? So that we can be
happy, so that our joy will be complete. Think about that.

Acts 18:23–28
Psalm 47:2–3,8–9,10
John 16:23b–28

Beloved, if God so loved us,
we also must love one another.
—1 JOHN 4:11

Love is not a feeling; love is a decision. We are loved by
God, so we must also love. There is no condition to this
proposition. God has loved us, and we must love in turn.
There is no kingdom, no promised afterlife, no eternal reality
with the Lord without choosing to love, and to love
unselfishly and unconditionally, as God has loved us. The
challenge is not to overthink things. If there is a question,
the answer is love. If there is a problem, the solution is love.
If there is a task, it's completed by love. We were created by
love to love; that is the meaning and purpose of our lives.

Acts 1:15–17,20a,20c–26
1 John 4:11–16
Psalm 103:1–2, 11–12, 19–20
John 17:11b–19
In some Provinces the celebration of Ascension is transferred to the Seventh Sunday of Easter

Monday

MAY 13

• OUR LADY OF FATIMA •

*[Jesus said,] "I have told you this so that you might have peace in me.
In the world you will have trouble,
but take courage, I have conquered the world."*
—JOHN 16:33

On this day, the church celebrates the Marian apparitions
that took place in Portugal, near Fatima, during the First
World War. Mary appeared to three poor shepherd children
with a series of messages. While extraordinary events
surrounded the appearances at Fatima, once Mary got the
world's attention, she wanted to make sure that we do three
simple things: pray for peace, do penance, and look to her
son for the salvation of our troubled world. Over the ninety
years since those original appearances, tens of millions of
pilgrims have visited the Shrine of Fatima to do just that.

Acts 19:1–8
Psalm 68:2–3ab,4–5acd,6–7ab
John 16:29–33

⇒ 163 ⇐

*[Jesus said,] "It was not you who chose me, but I who chose you
and appointed you to go and bear fruit that will remain,
so that whatever you ask the Father in my name he may give you.
This I command you: love one another."*
—JOHN 15:16–17

The church honors St. Matthias on this day. He is the only
apostle not chosen by Jesus personally. He was chosen to
replace Judas when Peter decided that someone who had
been with them since the beginning should fill the position.
According to tradition, Matthias traveled from Jerusalem to
Turkey and the Caspian Sea area, near modern-day Russia,
and brought many souls to the Lord. He is the patron saint of
carpenters, tailors, and, interestingly, alcoholics.

Acts 1:15–17,20–26
Psalm 113:1–2,3–4,5–6,7–8
John 15:9–17

_[Jesus said,] "They do not belong to the world
any more than I belong to the world."_
—JOHN 17:16

These are Jesus' words as he prays to his Father for his
disciples, whom he will be leaving soon. What does it mean
that "they do not belong to the world"? I believe that for
those of us who follow Jesus, while we do live in the here and
now, there is also a part of us that lives in the eternal
presence of the Lord who created us, and this is our heavenly
home, our forever home, and Jesus doesn't want us to
forget that.

Acts 20:28–38
Psalm 68:29–30,33–35a,35bc–36ab
John 17:11b–19

Thursday

MAY 16

You will show me the path to life.
—PSALM 16:11

There's a story from Jewish folklore of a good man with a
good wife and home, but who wishes to find paradise. So, he
sets out one day and walks far from home. His feet are sore;
he takes off his shoes and points them in the direction he'll
walk in the morning. Then he builds a fire, eats dinner, and
falls asleep. That night, an angel comes and turns his shoes in
the opposite direction. As he's walking the next day, he
notices things becoming more familiar. Then he spots his
wife and his home in the distance. His heart becomes full,
and he realizes in an instant that he has discovered exactly
what he had set out to find.

Acts 22:30; 23:6–11
Psalm 16:1–2a and 5,7–8,9–10,11
John 17:20–26

Friday

MAY 17

"Do you love me?" and [Peter] said to him,
"Lord, you know everything; you know that I love you."
—JOHN 21:17

It's not enough to know something; sometimes we need to
hear it. My mother was dying in a nursing home from
COVID-19. It was at the height of the epidemic. I couldn't
be with her and was feeling overwhelmed. My wife suggested
I call the nursing home and ask them to move my mother's
bed to the window so I could see her one last time. We drove
to the nursing home. I looked through her window. She saw
me and smiled from her bed. I said, "I love you." She raised
up a little, and said, "Not as much as I love you." She died
three days later, her final words a lasting blessing.

Acts 25:13b–21
Psalm 103:1–2,11–12,19–20ab
John 21:15–19

Saturday

MAY 18

• ST. JOHN I, POPE AND MARTYR •

The LORD is in his holy temple.
—PSALM 11:4

Reason #17 for Going to Church

I traveled a great deal in my last job, all over the country in fact. I used a terrific app called Mass Times. You punch in your zip code, and it will tell you where and when there is a Mass nearby. One of the awesome things about attending Mass on the road is that no matter where you are, with few exceptions, the service will be almost exactly like the service in your home parish. So, while you may be a thousand miles from your home, with people you don't know, when it comes to worshipping the Lord at Mass, you *are* home.

Acts 28:16–20,30–31
Psalm 11:4,5 and 7
John 21:20–25

Sunday

MAY 19

• PENTECOST SUNDAY •

In the same way, the Spirit too comes to the aid of our weakness;
for we do not know how to pray as we ought,
but the Spirit himself intercedes with inexpressible groanings.
—ROMANS 8:26

St. Paul writes in his letter to the church in Rome that all of creation is groaning with the labor pains of bringing forth the new world in Christ. He urges us to call upon the Holy Spirit to intercede on our behalf as we do this hard but necessary work. Think of the Holy Spirit as the midwife of our spiritual transformation.

VIGIL:
Genesis 11:1–9 or Exodus 19:3–8a,16–20b
or Ezekiel 37:1–4 or Joel 3:1–5
Psalm 104:1–2,24,35,27–28,29,30
Romans 8:22–27
John 7:37–39

DAY:
Acts 2:1–11
Psalm 104:1,24,29–30,31,34
1 Corinthians 12:3b–7,12–13 or
Galatians 5:16–25
John 20:19–23 or 15:26–27; 16:12–15

Monday

MAY 20

• THE BLESSED VIRGIN MARY, MOTHER OF THE CHURCH •

*Standing by the cross of Jesus were his mother
and his mother's sister, Mary the wife of Clopas,
and Mary of Magdala.*
—JOHN 19:25

Some years ago, I had the great blessing to work with one of
the most talented and I believe best Catholic writers of our
time. She has told her amazing story in her own words in
several compelling books. During the course of our work
together, I asked her how she had survived the many trials
and tribulations she had been through. She said to me,
without pause, "By clinging to the foot of the Cross every
day." I have taken her words to heart, and joined her, at the
foot of the Cross.

Genesis 3:9–15, 20 or Acts 1:12–14
Psalm 87:1–2, 3 and 5, 6–7
John 19:25–34

Tuesday

MAY 21

• ST. CHRISTOPHER MAGALLANES, PRIEST, AND COMPANIONS, MARTYRS •

Draw near to God, and he will draw near to you.
—JAMES 4:8

Faith is a journey, one we embark upon every day. God wants us to take a step forward in faith toward him. It can be a small step. It can be a tentative step. It doesn't matter because God will meet us where we are. The truth of our faith journey is that where we start is not nearly as important as where we end up.

James 4:1–10
Psalm 55:7–8,9–10a,10b–11a,23
Mark 9:30–37

Wednesday

MAY 22

• ST. RITA OF CASCIA, RELIGIOUS •

Yet in no way can a man redeem himself,
or pay his own ransom to God;
Too high is the price to redeem one's life.
—PSALM 49:8–9

Our lives have been redeemed by the death and resurrection
of our Lord Jesus. Our ransom paid with his blood. It would
be impossible for us to pay the steep price he has already
paid; however, it is possible to accept the gift he's given us
through the cross. The cross is the question the Father asks
of the Son. Jesus answered the Father with his life. The cross
is not merely a symbol; it is the defining truth of the faithful.
The Cross demands a response from each of us, and that
response is, "Yes, Lord."

James 4:13–17
Psalm 49:2–3,6–7,8–10,11
Mark 9:38–40

Thursday
MAY 23

Come now, you rich, weep and wail over your impending miseries.
—JAMES 5:1

It's worth noting that Scripture does not think much of worldly wealth and rich people in general. I'm not sure who said that if you wonder what God thinks of rich people, look at who has money. The truth is, though, almost all of us would like a little more money. But a lot of money? I am not sure that would be good. It's a cliché to hear stories of suddenly wealthy lottery winners who end up miserable and poor. That's not to say that life with money isn't easier than life without, but Jesus does say a rich person will not find it easy getting into heaven. So perhaps it's a matter of priorities. As for me, I'd like to get to heaven.

James 5:1–6
Psalm 49:14–15ab,15cd–16,17–18,19–20
Mark 9:41–50

But above all, my brothers and sisters, do not swear.
—JAMES 5:12

When I read the above passage, I felt a twinge of guilt. I do swear, sadly, but not as much as I used to. I'm working on trying not to swear at all, but it's a hard habit to break. I could take issue with how unrealistic it is never to swear, but I know a lot of good people who don't swear at all, so that's a poor argument. It's really a matter of control, and maybe character. I know I can control what I say. Also, what does it say about me when I do swear? Nothing good, I'm afraid. So, consider this my pledge to you, dear reader:
no more swearing!

James 5:9–12
Psalm 103:1–2,3–4,8–9,11–12
Mark 10:1–12

Saturday

MAY 25

• ST. BEDE THE VENERABLE, PRIEST AND DOCTOR OF THE CHURCH •
ST. GREGORY VII, POPE • ST. MARY MAGDALENE DE' PAZZI, VIRGIN •

The fervent prayer of a righteous person is very powerful.
—JAMES 5:16

I have a friend named Bert, and he's a good man. In fact, I would say he is a holy man. Whenever I need prayers, I call Bert. I'm not the only one—lots of people ask Bert to pray for them. So many people ask him for prayers, he has to keep a list, and it's a long list. He prays every day, for all of us. I'm grateful knowing Bert is there, praying for me and others in the world. I hope you have someone like Bert in your life, or that you're a Bert for others.

James 5:13–20
Psalm 141:1–2,3 and 8
Mark 10:13–16

[Jesus said,] "And behold, I am with you always,
until the end of the age."
—MATTHEW 28:20B

This is the last passage from the Gospel of Matthew. Jesus
has just given the disciples his final instructions to follow
upon his final leaving. But that last thing he says is
important: even though he is leaving, he promises to be with
them (and us) always. In ancient Greek, *always* is translated
as "the whole of every day." Then Jesus adds "until the end of
the age." So, what he is actually telling the disciples (and us)
is that he will be with them (and us) every moment, of every
day, until the end of time.

Deuteronomy 4:32–34,39–40
Psalm 33:4–5,6,9,18–19,20,22 (12b)
Romans 8:14–17
Matthew 28:16–20

Jesus, looking at him, loved him and said to him,
"You are lacking in one thing.
Go, sell what you have, and give to the poor
and you will have treasure in heaven; then come, follow me."
—MARK 10:21

I've always had a soft spot for the wealthy young man in this story. He obviously believed that it's possible to have everything. The one thing he lacked was the knowledge that ultimately what we need can come only in the form of a gift.

That gift is grace, and it comes from God. Upon our acceptance of that gift, we are forever transformed. I have no doubt Jesus smiled sadly as the young man walked away.

1 Peter 1:3–9
Psalm 111:1–2,5–6,9 and 10c
Mark 10:17–27

Tuesday

MAY 28

But, as he who called you is holy,
be holy yourselves in every aspect of your conduct,
for it is written, Be holy because I am holy.
—1 PETER 1:15–16

Our modern secular world has robbed many of us of a greater
sense of purpose and meaning, leaving us empty and
unsatisfied. We need an organizing principle, a guiding
influence to chart our course. What better principle or
influence than becoming holy? Becoming holy means to
become good, to be righteous, to love and follow God. The
good news is that our holiness is strengthened by his
holiness. He calls us to *"be holy because I am holy"*
(emphasis added).

1 Peter 1:10–16
Psalm 98:1,2–3ab,3cd–4
Mark 10:28–31

Wednesday

MAY 29

*[Jesus said,] "[T]he Son of Man did not come to be served but to serve
and to give his life as a ransom for many."*
—MARK 10:45

Our happiness in this life does not come from the absence of
trouble but from the strength to persevere when trouble
comes, because it *will* come. God shows us the way to
overcome those things we know we cannot overcome alone
but can overcome with God's help. The great mystery at the
heart of our faith is that the Lord of Light chooses to help
each of us; to befriend, to accompany, and yes, to serve each
of us. It was for this that he gave his life.

1 Peter 1:18–25
Psalm 147:12–13,14–15,19–20
Mark 10:32–45

Thursday

MAY 30

Jesus said to him in reply, "What do you want me to do for you?"
The blind man replied to him, "Master, I want to see."
Jesus told him, "Go your way; your faith has saved you."
Immediately he received his sight
and followed him on the way.
—MARK 10:51–52

Jesus knew the blind man was blind. He also knew the blind man would ask him to heal his blindness. But still, Jesus asks him, "What do you want me to do for you?" After Jesus heals the man's blindness, he tells the man that his faith has saved him. Not "your faith has allowed you to see," but "your faith has saved you." Jesus isn't simply restoring the man's sight, he's saving his soul. Jesus already knows what we want and what we need, but he wants us to ask him.

1 Peter 2:2–5,9–12
Psalm 100:2,3,4,5
Mark 10:46–52

Friday

MAY 31

• THE VISITATION OF THE BLESSED VIRGIN MARY •

Rejoice in hope,
endure in affliction,
persevere in prayer.
—ROMANS 12:12

Thank goodness Mary was not a control freak. She was an unmarried virgin; an angel had told her she was pregnant by the Lord. When she decided to visit Elizabeth to get away from home for a little while, she finds that her elderly relative is pregnant and already knows that Mary's pregnant, not to mention that Elizabeth's husband, Zechariah, is mysteriously mute. Meanwhile, she is contending with the growing awareness she's carrying the Messiah. What does Mary do? Exactly what St. Paul suggests: she rejoices in hope, endures in affliction, and perseveres in prayer. Mary may have been young, but she trusted the Lord and knew he was in charge.

Zephaniah 3:14–18a or Romans 12:9–16
Isaiah 12:2–3,4bcd,5–6
Luke 1:39–56

Saturday
JUNE 1
• ST. JUSTIN, MARTYR •

Build yourselves up in your most holy faith;
pray in the Holy Spirit.
Keep yourselves in the love of God
and wait for the mercy of our Lord Jesus Christ
that leads to eternal life.
—JUDE 20–21

As I mentioned earlier, I set aside about an hour each
morning to pray. As Jesus encourages us to do, I have become
more mindful of asking the Holy Spirit to join me in my
prayer. Over the years, I've come to believe the Holy Spirit
helps boost my prayers like a special, spiritual, high-speed
HD signal beaming them right up to heaven.

Jude 17,20b–25
Psalm 63:2,3–4,5–6
Mark 11:27–33

How shall I make a return to the LORD
for all the good he has done for me?
—PSALM 116:12

On this day the church celebrates the real presence of Jesus
in both the liturgy of the Eucharist and in the church itself.
Not merely a symbolic presence, but a real, true, and
substantial presence, best captured by these words from St.
Patrick: *Christ with me, Christ before me, Christ behind me, Christ in*
me, Christ beneath me, Christ above me, Christ on my right, Christ on
my left, Christ when I lie down, Christ when I sit down, Christ
when I arise.

Exodus 24:3–8
Psalm 116:12–13,15–16,17–18 (13)
Hebrews 9:11–15
Mark 14:12–16,22–26

Jesus began to speak to the chief priests, the scribes,
and the elders in parables.
"A man planted a vineyard."
—MARK 12:1

Jesus spoke in parables because the message he was sharing
was often best delivered in story form. Parables take a high
degree of creative thought and symbolic logic. If I had been
with Jesus and he asked my help with his teachings, I might
have suggested he simply say, "Be mindful of the seeds you
plant today; they produce the crops you harvest tomorrow."
But Jesus was smart; while it's easy to forget an aphorism, it's
almost impossible to forget a good story, especially one that
begins like "The kingdom of heaven may be likened to a man
who sowed good seed in his field" (Matthew 13:24).

2 Peter 1:2–7
Psalm 91:1–2,14–15b,15c–16
Mark 12:1–12

Tuesday

JUNE 4

*For a thousand years in your sight
are as yesterday.*
—PSALM 90:4

While each of us is a necessary part of this world while we're in it, this world will go on without us. Our lives are relatively short in the span of God's sight. So, our challenge is to live good and meaningful lives with the time we have been given, to do something with our time here and not just talk about doing something. Because when it's all said and done, we don't want to have said more than we've done.

2 Peter 3:12–15a,17–18
Psalm 90:2,3–4,10,14 and 16
Mark 12:13–17

Wednesday

JUNE 5

• ST. BONIFACE, BISHOP AND MARTYR •

*Bear your share of hardship for the Gospel
with the strength that comes from God.*
—2 TIMOTHY 1:8

We will always face some hardship—but the hardship we encounter need not diminish us or leave us feeling insignificant. We can choose to let the hardship draw us closer to the Lord in shared suffering. We can, as Sister Margaret Mary said in parochial school, "Bring it to the cross." There, with the Lord, we can embrace our hardship with the strength that comes from the grace of God. Our acceptance of the hardship can help our spirits grow larger than the hardship endured, and the tenderness of our shared devotion with the Lord can transform and heal our souls.

2 Timothy 1:1–3,6–12
Psalm 123:1b–2ab,2cdef
Mark 12:18–27

JUNE 6

• ST. NORBERT, BISHOP •

And when Jesus saw that he answered with understanding,
he said to him,
"You are not far from the Kingdom of God."
—MARK 12:34

Jesus engages with a scribe who, unlike most of his fellow scribes, recognizes Jesus as the Messiah. This man—think of him as a modestly successful village lawyer—might be shunned and compromised by publicly acknowledging or following Jesus. Ultimately, we don't know what happens after his meeting with Jesus. But having Jesus pronounce him as being "not far from the kingdom of God" probably altered the trajectory of his comfortable, establishment life. Like others touched by Jesus, it would be wonderful to know what direction his life took after this encounter. Let's pray he is now with Jesus in the kingdom of God.

2 Timothy 2:8–15
Psalm 25:4–5ab,8–9,10 and 14
Mark 12:28–34

Friday

JUNE 7

• THE SACRED HEART OF JESUS •

To me, the very least of all the holy ones, this grace was given,
to preach to the Gentiles the inscrutable riches of Christ,
and to bring to light for all what is the plan of the mystery
hidden from ages past in God who created all things.
—EPHESIANS 3:8–9

Paul's language is vivid and compelling; it speaks to the
grandeur and majesty of Jesus as Paul understood him: "the
inscrutable riches of Christ . . . to bring to light for all what
is the plan of the mystery hidden from ages past." Paul's
enthusiasm for Jesus was/is contagious. He makes you want
to know more. Whatever you think about St. Paul, he got
people excited to learn more about Jesus, and his words still
do today.

Hosea 11:1,3–4,8c–9
Isaiah 12:2–3,4,5–6 (3)
Ephesians 3:8–12,14–19
John 19:31–37

I have competed well;
I have finished the race; I have kept the faith.
—2 TIMOTHY 4:7

In 1969, Bob Wieland lost both legs stepping on a mortar while rescuing another soldier in Vietnam. Many people might have given up and accepted their injuries as limitations. Not Bob: in 1986, he completed the New York City Marathon in ninety-eight hours. Then in 2003, he finished the Los Angeles Marathon in 173 hours. He completed both races using only his arms and torso. He was asked how he did it. "It was done by the grace of God, one step at a time." Bob embodies 2 Timothy 4:7. He competed well, he finished the race, and he kept the faith.

2 Timothy 4:1–8
Psalm 71:8–9,14–15ab,16–17,22
Luke 2:41–51

For we know that if our earthly dwelling, a tent,
should be destroyed,
we have a building from God,
a dwelling not made with hands, eternal in heaven.
—2 CORINTHIANS 5:1

Recently, I was talking to a theologian about prayer and the early church, and we happened on the Apostles' Creed. She said that only two names are mentioned in the creed, Mary and Pontius Pilate. I hadn't thought about that and asked her about it. She said Mary had made a home, a dwelling for God on earth. Pilate tried to kill God, denying him a place on earth. Mary welcomed God, Pilate did not. These are our two possible responses to God. I'll never think about the Apostles' Creed the same way again.

Genesis 3:9–15
Psalm 130:1–2,3–4,5–6,7–8 (7bc)
2 Corinthians 4:13—5:1
Mark 3:20–35

Monday
JUNE 10

Blessed are the clean of heart,
for they will see God.
—MATTHEW 5:8

You can't see out of a dirty window, no matter how beautiful
the view. If your glasses are dirty, everything is hard to see,
so you need to wipe them. When you're driving, if your
windshield is dirty, you need to stop and clean it. Our hearts
are the eyes of our interior world, and we need to keep our
hearts clean so that we can see with an unfiltered, unclouded,
unobstructed view the love God has for us and all creation.

The sacrament of reconciliation is offered to us for this
express purpose, an opportunity to cleanse our hearts. If for
no other reason, let us have clean hearts so that, as Jesus says
in his Sermon on the Mount, we "will see God."

1 Kings 17:1–6
Psalm 121:1bc–2,3–4,5–6,7–8
Matthew 5:1–12

JUNE 11

• ST. BARNABAS, APOSTLE •

[Jesus said,] "You are the light of the world."
—MATTHEW 5:14

Jesus is speaking to his disciples when he says in Matthew's Gospel, "You are the light of the world." In John's Gospel, Jesus refers to himself as the "light of the world." I don't think the meaning is hard to discern here: Jesus is the light in a world that can often appear dark and unwelcoming. As followers of Jesus, we are to do what he came to do and light the way for others through our good works, our mercy, our compassion, our faith, and especially our love.

Acts 11:21b–26; 13:1–3
Psalm 98:1,2–3ab,3cd–4,5–6
Matthew 5:13–16

Wednesday

JUNE 12

The LORD's fire came down
and consumed the burnt offering, wood, stones, and dust,
and it lapped up the water in the trench.
Seeing this, all the people fell prostrate and said,
"The LORD is God! The LORD is God!"
—1 KINGS 18:38–39

I encourage you to take a moment and read 1 Kings, chapter 18. It's a chronicle of a battle between Yahweh's prophet Elijah and the prophets of Baal. It's a powerful story, with echoes of David versus Goliath. God's chosen people often appear fickle in their relationship to Yahweh in the early days of covenant. The great prophets are always trying to bring them back. Reading Scripture closely, it's remarkable how hard the Lord worked to prove his fealty, his devotion, his love for his chosen people. He still does.

1 Kings 18:20–39
Psalm 16:1b–2ab,4,5ab and 8,11
Matthew 5:17–19

Thursday

JUNE 13

[Jesus said,] "I tell you,
unless your righteousness surpasses that
of the scribes and Pharisees,
you will not enter into the Kingdom of heaven."
—MATTHEW 5:20

This is Jesus speaking to his disciples. He is telling them,
Unless you are more righteous than the experts in their laws
and their religious teachers and leaders, you cannot enter the
kingdom of heaven. Translating this for our times, Jesus is
saying, Unless we are more law-abiding than the legal
establishment and more faithful than our religious leaders, we
will not enter heaven. This tells us two things about Jesus.
First, he wants us to hold ourselves to a higher standard in all
things. Second, he has little respect for the powers that be.

1 Kings 18:41–46
Psalm 65:10,11,12–13
Matthew 5:20–26

Hear, O LORD, the sound of my call;
have pity on me, and answer me.
—PSALM 27:7

Psalm 27 is a prayer of lament. The psalmist is calling upon the Lord to hear him, to see him, to answer him in his distress. This is a pure form of prayer found throughout the psalms and elsewhere in Scripture. It is also an effective form of prayer when we are suffering and going through difficult times. Praying the psalms can bring us solace and consolation. We are not alone in our distress; we are not alone in our hopes that God will hear us. Try reading/praying the psalms with an open and listening heart. You may be surprised how effective this ancient form of prayer can be for our troubled modern souls.

1 Kings 19:9a,11–16
Psalm 27:7–8a,8b–9abc,13–14
Matthew 5:27–32

Saturday

JUNE 15

[Jesus said,] "Let your 'Yes' mean 'Yes,' and your 'No' mean 'No.'"
—MATTHEW 5:37

Jesus is speaking to his disciples and offering them his take
on a range of subjects—anger, divorce, adultery,
retaliation—and in this passage he specifically addresses
swearing, oaths, and the promises we make. Often, Jesus'
teachings upended the established social and religious order
and were seen as disruptive and radical. But not so here, I
believe. When I read this, I hear Jesus saying, "Don't say yes
unless you mean yes, and don't say no unless you mean no."
Mean what you say and say what you mean and keep it
simple. Pretty straightforward.

1 Kings 19:19–21
Psalm 16:1b–2a and 5,7–8,9–10
Matthew 5:33–37

Sunday

JUNE 16

• ELEVENTH SUNDAY IN ORDINARY TIME •

With many such parables
he spoke the word to them as they were able to understand it.
Without parables he did not speak to them,
but to his own disciples he explained everything in private.
—MARK 4:33–34

Jesus is a master teacher, and he uses stories to great effect.
The crowds following Jesus come and go, so he needs to
make his points in the most memorable, lasting ways he can.
Using parables often accomplishes this best. Because the
disciples are with Jesus all the time, they learn much by
simply being around him. But knowing they will teach and
preach in his name after he is gone, he empowers them with
the truth within the truth of his teachings.

Ezekiel 17:22–24
Psalm 92:2–3,13–14,15–16
2 Corinthians 5:6–10
Mark 4:26–34

Hearken to my words, O LORD,
attend to my sighing.
—PSALM 5:2

I sigh a lot these days; it's probably the sheer repetition of struggles, challenges, and the never-ending problems of getting older and simply enduring life as it comes. Carl Jung said that *"the greatest and most important problems of life are fundamentally insoluble. They can never be solved but only outgrown."* I think this is partly true. For me, I also believe that, with God's help, the insurmountable problems of life shrink in time and relevance as we grow in faith. I used to say, "Okay Lord, let's do this." Now, when struggles come, I hear God say, "Okay Joe, let's do this." Wisdom is knowing that God's got your back. That doesn't mean things won't get hard, but when they inevitably do, I'm not alone.

1 Kings 21:1–16
Psalm 5:2–3ab,4b–6a,6b–7
Matthew 5:38–42

Tuesday

JUNE 18

Jesus said to his disciples:
"You have heard that it was said,
You shall love your neighbor and hate your enemy.
But I say to you, love your enemies
and pray for those who persecute you."
—MATTHEW 5:43–44

This is probably the hardest teaching in the Bible: Love your enemies. In order to love our enemies, really love them, we need to see them as fellow human beings who struggle and strive just as we do. We need to forgive them. We can't allow hate to dehumanize them. It's easy to hate from afar; it's easy to hate what's different. Jesus is asking us to find that common ground of humanity that we all share, however different we might appear, and to choose love. In choosing love, we transform hate, and ourselves.

1 Kings 21:17–29
Psalm 51:3–4,5–6ab,11 and 16
Matthew 5:43–48

Wednesday

JUNE 19

• ST. ROMUALD, ABBOT •

Jesus said to his disciples:
"Take care not to perform righteous deeds
in order that people may see them."
—MATTHEW 6:1

Jesus goes to great lengths to persuade the disciples to be helpful, to do good and be good. But he urges them to do works of charity, to pray, to fast, and to do all of it without anyone knowing. He tells them to pray in secret, in a closed room, alone. He tells them not to let anyone else know who they help with their charity. He tells them not to let anyone know they are fasting. But then he reassures them that everything they do in secret, his father sees and will repay, no doubt also in secret. I wonder what Jesus would think of our smartphone-obsessed, selfie-saturated, social-media-dominated world?

2 Kings 2:1,6–14
Psalm 31:20,21,24
Matthew 6:1–6,16–18

Thursday

JUNE 20

[Jesus said,] "Your Father knows what you need before you ask him."
—MATTHEW 6:8

The above passage is what Jesus says just before he teaches the disciples the Our Father. In the Our Father, Jesus offers six key points:

God's kingdom will eventually come to earth.

Stay in the perfect will of God.

God's kingdom will be the only one that endures.

God will provide what we need in this life.

Forgive others and ourselves.

Ask for God's help with temptation and evil.

As significant as these six truths are, I think what he says before giving us the Our Father is also of great importance: God already knows what we need, even before we ask him. Which is why the next best prayer to the Our Father may simply be "Thank you, Lord."

Sirach 48:1–14
Psalm 97:1–2,3–4,5–6,7
Matthew 6:7–15

"For where your treasure is, there also will your heart be."
—MATTHEW 6:21

Aloysius was born in Italy in 1568. He was a devout, virtuous, and prayerful young man. Against the will of his father, he joined the Jesuits at the age of eighteen. From a wealthy family, he gave up his right to an inheritance. In 1591, when plague broke out in Rome where Aloysius was then living, he volunteered to serve plague victims in the hospital, eventually coming down with the plague himself. Aloysius predicted he would die on the Feast of Corpus Christi. On the morning of Corpus Christi, he seemed fine but grew weaker throughout the day. He died just before midnight. He was only twenty-three. In 1726, he was canonized as one of the Church's youngest saints.

2 Kings 11:1–4,9–18,20
Psalm 132:11,12,13–14,17–18
Matthew 6:19–23

Saturday

JUNE 22

"Can any of you by worrying add a single moment to your life-span?"
—MATTHEW 6:27

Worrying is often born out of an unconscious need to control
outcomes. But a simple reflection of where our lives have
taken us over the last five, ten years, will demonstrate how
little control we've had over those outcomes. Granted, we
can choose, and hopefully we choose well the most
important aspects of life, but if we're honest, there is little we
really control. Sometimes what we never wanted or expected
turns out to be exactly what we needed. So, stop worrying,
start living, and have faith that God has things well in hand,
because he does.

2 Chronicles 24:17–25
Psalm 89:4–5,29–30,31–32,33–34
Matthew 6:24–34

Sunday

JUNE 23

• TWELFTH SUNDAY IN ORDINARY TIME •

So whoever is in Christ is a new creation:
the old things have passed away;
behold, new things have come.
—2 CORINTHIANS 5:17

Paul is telling us the profound truth of following Jesus: we are reborn with him and become new creations. The old self passes away, and the love of Christ impels us into new beings. Perhaps no one has expressed this truth quite so elegantly as John Newton, the writer of "Amazing Grace":

I once was lost, but now I'm found,
Was blind but now I see.

Job 38:1,8–11
Psalm 107:23–24,25–26,28–29,30–31 (1b)
2 Corinthians 5:14–17
Mark 4:35–41

Monday
JUNE 24
• THE NATIVITY OF ST. JOHN THE BAPTIST •

Beloved:
Although you have not seen Jesus Christ you love him;
even though you do not see him now yet believe in him,
you rejoice with an indescribable and glorious joy,
as you attain the goal of your faith, the salvation of your souls.
—1 PETER 1:8–9

Today, the church celebrates the birth of John the Baptist. I
was in college, studying Scripture, when I first saw *Godspell*.
But that initial scene in the movie with John in the park
fountain, singing "Prepare ye the way of the Lord" helped
introduce me to the spirit of John the Baptist in a way none
of my classes ever did.

VIGIL:
Jeremiah 1:4–10
Psalm 71:1–2,3–4a,5–6ab,15ab and 17
1 Peter 1:8–12
Luke 1:5–17

DAY:
Isaiah 49:1–6
Psalm 139:1b–3,13–14ab,14c–15
Acts 13:22–26
Luke 1:57–66,80

Tuesday

JUNE 25

[Jesus said,] "Enter through the narrow gate;
for the gate is wide and the road broad that leads to destruction,
and those who enter through it are many."
—MATTHEW 7:13–14

What is Jesus telling us by inviting us to enter through the narrow gate, while acknowledging how difficult it is? I'm not going to answer that question but instead suggest you don't avoid or be afraid to wrestle with the challenging lessons Jesus teaches. It takes time to learn and be transformed by difficult truths. Don't shortchange your struggle; lean into your questions, listen for the wisdom of God, live in his presence, embrace your faith. It's alright to have to work from uncertainty and doubt to insight and understanding; that's how you'll find the real answers.

2 Kings 19:9b–11,14–21,31–35a,36
Psalm 48:2–3ab,3cd–4,10–11
Matthew 7:6,12–14

*Give me discernment, that I may observe your law
and keep it with all my heart.*
—PSALM 119:34

Discernment is a way of making good choices; weighing your options; considering your feelings and emotions, outcomes, and consequences. Take your time, and make an informed decision rather than a rushed, irrational one. When you look at a person's life, good or not so good, you'll see it's their choices that often informed the trajectory of their lives. The simplest way to make better choices is to invite God into your decision making. Take a quiet moment and share your deliberations with God. Then listen with an open heart. God will never mislead you. Make your pros and cons lists, consult your trusted advisors, but pray, and include God in your process. That will prove to be your best decision.

2 Kings 22:8–13; 23:1–3
Psalm 119:33, 34, 35, 36, 37, 40
Matthew 7:15–20

JUNE 27

• ST. CYRIL OF ALEXANDRIA, BISHOP AND DOCTOR OF THE CHURCH •

O God, the nations have come into your inheritance;
they have defiled your holy temple,
they have laid Jerusalem in ruins.
They have left the corpses of your servants
as food to the birds of heaven,
the flesh of your faithful ones to the beasts of the earth.
—PSALM 79:1–3

Reading the Old Testament can sometimes be a real struggle.
Yahweh often appears vindictive and indifferent to his
people. There is a quote, attributed to St. Theresa of Ávila,
about God: "You have so few friends because you treat them
so badly." Of course, the Old Testament is followed by a
great sequel, and I especially like the hero in that story.

2 Kings 24:8–17
Psalm 79:1b–2,3–5,8,9
Matthew 7:21–29

Friday

JUNE 28

• ST. IRENAEUS, BISHOP AND MARTYR •

When Jesus came down from the mountain,
great crowds followed him.
And then a leper approached, did him homage, and said,
"Lord, if you wish, you can make me clean."
He stretched out his hand, touched him, and said,
"I will do it. Be made clean."
His leprosy was cleansed immediately.
—MATTHEW 8:1–3

Today, we celebrate the feast of St. Irenaeus (c. 125–c. 202).
He wrote, *"The glory of God is the human person fully alive."*
When the leper in today's Gospel asks Jesus to heal him,
what he says is "make me clean." The leper's faith was such
that the glory of God not only cured his leprosy but restored
and made him fully alive.

2 Kings 25:1–12
Psalm 137:1–2,3,4–5,6
Matthew 8:1–4

Saturday

JUNE 29

• ST. PETER AND ST. PAUL, APOSTLES •

The Lord will rescue me from every evil threat
and will bring me safe to his heavenly Kingdom.
To him be glory forever and ever. Amen.
—2 TIMOTHY 4:18

Today, the church celebrates the feast of the two great apostles. Both were executed in Rome upon orders of the emperor Nero. Peter was crucified upside down, at his request, because he said he was not worthy to be crucified as the Lord was. Paul, being a Roman citizen, was beheaded. Within three hundred years, the empire that executed Peter and Paul became the center of their movement. Today, large churches sit upon the sites where both saints died.

VIGIL:	DAY:
Acts 3:1–10	Acts 12:1–11
Psalm 19:2–3,4–5	Psalm 34:2–3,4–5,6–7,8–9
Galatians 1:11–20	2 Timothy 4:6–8,17–18
John 21:15–19	Matthew 16:13–19

God did not make death,
nor does he rejoice in the destruction of the living.
—WISDOM 1:13

The truth is, you and I know far too little of the mystery that is life and death. But there is one who knows, and that's God. So, in the face of the mystery, we put our trust in God the Father. The Father who gave us Jesus. The Father who gave us life. The Father who guides our lives, and the Father who waits to embrace us, not in death, but in life eternal.

Wisdom 1:13–15; 2:23–24
Psalm 30:2,4,5–6,11,12,13 (2a)
2 Corinthians 8:7,9,13–15
Mark 5:21–43

Monday

JULY 1

• ST. JUNÍPERO SERRA, PRIEST •

Another of his disciples said to him,
"Lord, let me go first and bury my father."
But Jesus answered him, "Follow me,
and let the dead bury their dead."
—MATTHEW 8:21–22

Jesus sounds harsh, almost insensitive. But he has been busy teaching and healing nonstop. This person is a disciple, so he has accepted the invitation to follow Jesus, and all that entails. Also, burial customs at that time could include staying with a dying person for some time before they died. After this exchange, Jesus gets in a boat and promptly falls asleep. In fact, he is so exhausted, he is sleeping through a storm when the disciples wake him in a panic. Harsh, insensitive? Jesus was tired, busy, maybe a little impatient, but should we be surprised?

Amos 2:6–10,13–16
Psalm 50:16bc–17,18–19,20–21,22–23
Matthew 8:18–22

At dawn I bring my plea expectantly before you.
—PSALM 5:4B

Each morning, I have an elaborate prayer ritual, which I have written about previously. What I have not mentioned is my prayer map. I used to have a prayer list, and before that I kept a prayer journal. Essentially, if someone asked me to pray for them, I would add their name and petition to a list or journal page. This became cumbersome and messy, with a lot of adding and crossing out. Eventually, I created a memory technique I call the prayer map. With a visual of the world in my mind, I travel to the cities, states, and countries where those I wish to pray for reside. It works, though I wish I could accumulate frequent flyer miles for my inner travels.

Amos 3:1–8; 4:11–12
Psalm 5:4b–6a,6b–7,8
Matthew 8:23–27

Then he said to Thomas, "Put your finger here and see my hands,
and bring your hand and put it into my side,
and do not be unbelieving, but believe."
Thomas answered and said to him, "My Lord and my God!"
Jesus said to him, "Have you come to believe because you have seen me?
Blessed are those who have not seen and have believed."
—JOHN 20:27–29

Do you ever think that a book might not be necessary to read because the title is so good it probably tells the whole story? Wayne Dyer wrote a best-selling book published in 1989 called *You'll See It When You Believe It.* This is a book St. Thomas might have benefited from, but the truth is, we are all a little St. Thomas, struggling to become a little more Wayne Dyer.

Ephesians 2:19–22
Psalm 117:1bc,2
John 20:24–29

Thursday

JULY 4

• INDEPENDENCE DAY •

[Jesus said,] "Which is easier, to say, 'Your sins are forgiven,'
or to say, 'Rise and walk'?"
—MATTHEW 9:5

Jesus again encounters hostile officials who try to trap him in
blasphemy when he claims he is God. But Jesus neatly
sidesteps their ideological arguments by offering an elegant
rhetorical rebuttal: "Okay, so is it easier to say your sins are
forgiven or to say rise and walk?" Well, both are easy to say,
but only God can make either happen, and Jesus does. Jesus
shows the scribes and the crowds the power of God, but
what might be lost in the spectacle of all this is the greater
gift received by the paralytic who was healed. He not only
could walk again, but Jesus forgave his sins, restored his soul,
and made him whole, both within and without.

Amos 7:10–17
Psalm 19:8,9,10,11
Matthew 9:1–8
or, for Independence Day, any readings from the Mass "For the Country or a City,"
(882–886), or the Mass "For Peace and Justice" (887–891)

Friday

JULY 5

• ST. ELIZABETH OF PORTUGAL • ST. ANTHONY MARY ZACCARIA, PRIEST •

With all my heart I seek you;
let me not stray from your commands.
—PSALM 119:10

It is reassuring to learn that we do not come to God by doing
it right, by following the rules, or by being perfect. We come
to God through our failings, our flaws, and our faults.
Otherwise, instead of falling in love with God and accepting
his enduring grace and mercy, we may fall in love with
ourselves, mistakenly believing we had anything to do with
our own salvation.

Amos 8:4–6,9–12
Psalm 119:2,10,20,30,40,131
Matthew 9:9–13

Kindness and truth shall meet;
justice and peace shall kiss.
—PSALM 85:11

The story of Maria Goretti is a sad, brutal story, especially as
the world sees it. But through the lens of faith, it becomes a
magnificent chronicle of forgiveness and redemption. Maria
was attacked and stabbed repeatedly, and Alessandro, the
man who attacked and attempted to rape her, was eventually
captured. Unrepentant and in prison for decades, he had a
dream that changed everything. He was in a garden with
Maria, and she gave him flowers; looking down, he saw they
burned his hands. Finally released, he sought Maria's mother
to beg her forgiveness, and she did forgive him. Alessandro
became a lay Capuchin, living a quiet life of prayer and
gardening. As an old man, he was at St. Peter's Basilica for
Maria's canonization.

Amos 9:11–15
Psalm 85:9ab and 10,11–12,13–14
Matthew 9:14–17

Sunday

JULY 7

• FOURTEENTH SUNDAY IN ORDINARY TIME •

Therefore, I am content with weaknesses, insults,
hardships, persecutions, and constraints,
for the sake of Christ;
for when I am weak, then I am strong.
—2 CORINTHIANS 12:10

The key words here are "for the sake of Christ." Paul had his
entire life turned upside down and given new meaning by his
encounter with the risen Christ on the road to Damascus.
The greatest persecutor of his time had become the greatest
evangelist of his time. For Paul, suffering for the sake of
Christ only drew him nearer to Christ. His weakness allowed
God's strength to transform him. Paul was also convinced
that Jesus' return was imminent, and everything Paul did was
to make ready for Christ's reappearance. For Paul, it was
never about himself; it was always, and only, about Jesus.

Ezekiel 2:2–5
Psalm 123:1–2,2,3–4
2 Corinthians 12:7–10
Mark 6:1–6

A woman suffering hemorrhages for twelve years came up behind him
and touched the tassel on his cloak.
She said to herself, "If only I can touch his cloak, I shall be cured."
Jesus turned around and saw her, and said,
"Courage, daughter! Your faith has saved you."
And from that hour the woman was cured.
—MATTHEW 9:20–22

Today's Gospel reading is about the power of faith. A father
believing that Jesus, by simply touching his daughter, can
bring her back from the dead. A long-suffering woman
believes she will be healed if she can simply touch the cloak
of Jesus as he walks by. Jesus does not disappoint, bringing
the young girl back to life and healing the woman. When we
have the courage to reach out in faith to Jesus,
miracles are possible.

Hosea 2:16,17c–18,21–22
Psalm 145:2–3,4–5,6–7,8–9
Matthew 9:18–26

Tuesday

JULY 9

• ST. AUGUSTINE ZHAO RONG, PRIEST, AND COMPANIONS, MARTYRS •

Our God is in heaven:
whatever he wills, he does.
—PSALM 115:3

Our task as believers is to align with the will of God. As Jesus taught in the Our Father, "Thy will be done, on earth as it is in heaven." The only way we can know the will of God is to pray. Prayer establishes the connection through which God speaks to us. Prayer is the bridge between heaven and earth. Jesus walked across that bridge and brought heaven's light to earth. The Holy Spirit keeps the channel open and continues to keep heaven's light bright for us. So, pray with abandonment. Pray unceasingly. Pray through your doubt. Pray as if your very life depends on it, because, in the end, it does.

Hosea 8:4–7,11–13
Psalm 115:3–4,5–6,7ab–8,9–10
Matthew 9:32–38

*[Jesus said,] "As you go, make this proclamation:
'The Kingdom of heaven is at hand.'"*
—MATTHEW 10:7

Jesus tells this to the Twelve before sending them out with
the power to cure every illness and drive out unclean spirits.
But what does "The kingdom of heaven is at hand" mean? I
believe Jesus is saying, "I am here now, and I have brought
the kingdom, and the power of the kingdom of heaven is
with me. It's here and it's now, it's all around you, and now it's
yours. Believe and act accordingly with the power I have
brought you from God the Father." Jesus has begun the great
restoration, repairing what has been broken and what only
he can fix. In our contemporary cultural parlance, Jesus is
saying to the Twelve, and us, "Game on!"

Hosea 10:1–3,7–8,12
Psalm 105:2–3,4–5,6–7
Matthew 10:1–7

Thursday

JULY 11

• ST. BENEDICT, ABBOT •

*[Jesus said,] "Whatever town or village you enter, look for a worthy person in it,
and stay there until you leave."*
—MATTHEW 10:11

St. Benedict, whose feast day the church celebrates on this day, lived fifteen hundred years ago and is most noted for creating the monastic community system that is still in place today. He is also noted for his classic book *The Rule of St. Benedict*. "Let everyone that comes be received as Christ" is one of the most quoted phrases from the Rule. Hospitality is practiced in every Benedictine monastery, and Benedictine hospitality goes well beyond the exercise of the warm reception of visitors. Hospitality for Benedict meant that every guest should be received and welcomed as if they were Jesus himself.

Hosea 11:1–4,8e–9
Psalm 80:2ac and 3b,15–16
Matthew 10:7–15

Let him who is wise understand these things;
let him who is prudent know them.
Straight are the paths of the LORD,
in them the just walk,
but sinners stumble in them.
—HOSEA 14:10

While this may have been written over eighteen hundred years ago, for a people who did not have the Internet, Netflix, iPhones, downloadable audiobooks, digital music, e-mail, texting—or even indoor plumbing, microwaves, planes, trains, or automobiles—it is what we call perennial wisdom. Wisdom that never grows old or changes with the times, unlike our latest technologies. Follow the ways of God. He will make straight our paths and upon them we will walk with confidence, purpose, and meaning. Stray off the paths of the Lord, and we will stumble and fall. True eighteen hundred years ago, true today.

Hosea 14:2–10
Psalm 51:3–4,8–9,12–13,14 and 17
Matthew 10:16–23

Saturday
JULY 13
• ST. HENRY •

[Jesus said,] "What I say to you in the darkness, speak in the light;
what you hear whispered, proclaim on the housetops."
—MATTHEW 10:27

Jesus is a God of intimate proximities—a God of whispers in
the night, and a God of rooftop proclamations. Jesus is not a
distant God. It is almost cliché to say that Jesus meets us
where we are, but the meaning in that statement is that Jesus
meets us where we are because he is right there with us. And
what is Jesus whispering to us in the dark of night, and what
does he want us to shout from the rooftops in the light of
day? That we are loved and he is with us always.

Isaiah 6:1–8
Psalm 93:1ab,1cd–2,5
Matthew 10:24–33

⇒ 224 ⇐

Blessed be the God and Father of our Lord Jesus Christ,
who has blessed us in Christ
with every spiritual blessing in the heavens,
as he chose us in him, before the foundation of the world,
to be holy and without blemish before him.
In love he destined us for adoption to himself
through Jesus Christ.
—EPHESIANS 1:3–6

St. Paul says that God the Father chose us before the world was formed, to be with him, and with Christ. He chose us to be adopted with Christ so we can be with God the Father in heaven and experience the gift of every spiritual blessing, forever. Consider this the next time you are feeling a little down or alone.

Amos 7:12–15
Psalm 85:9–10,11–12,13–14 (8)
Ephesians 1:3–14 or 1:3–10
Mark 6:7–13

• ST. BONAVENTURE, BISHOP AND DOCTOR OF THE CHURCH •

Jesus said to his Apostles:
"Do not think that I have come to bring peace upon the earth.
I have come to bring not peace but the sword."
—MATTHEW 10:34

This is one of the hard sayings of Jesus. I believe he wants us to wrestle with this and try to grasp it for ourselves. A sword cuts through things; it separates. In Jesus' time, a sword was both a weapon and a tool. Jesus came to share the kingdom of heaven, which he pointedly said was not of this world. His mission was to share what was not easily seen or perceived, and how do you do something like that? You cut away what obscures it, perhaps with something like a sword.

Isaiah 1:10–17
Psalm 50:8–9,16bc–17,21 and 23
Matthew 10:34—11:1

JULY  16

• OUR LADY OF MOUNT CARMEL •

Unless your faith is firm
you shall not be firm!
—ISAIAH 7:9

Life can be hard; faith is what gives us the strength to make it through. Frederick Buechner wrote that the story of each of us is in some measure the story of all of us. Just as the journey of each of us is in some measure the journey of all of us. Faith allows us to sense this larger connection that binds us all together. It is a faith born in perseverance and courage, mercy, and love. Let us keep the faith.

Isaiah 7:1–9
Psalm 48:2–3a,3b–4,5–6,7–8
Matthew 11:20–24

At that time Jesus exclaimed:
"I give praise to you, Father, Lord of heaven and earth,
for although you have hidden these things
from the wise and the learned
you have revealed them to the childlike."
—MATTHEW 11:25

Jesus often preached to intelligent people who failed to understand him or grasp who and what he was. I believe this is what he is referring to in this passage. Intelligence and education can hinder spiritual understanding. Judgment, cultural bias, and acquired intolerance for other points of view are all part of what happens to most of us by the time we are adults. Let us pray to become more open to wonder—like a child—and free of judgment, so that we see what the Lord has hidden right in front of us.

Isaiah 10:5–7,13b–16
Psalm 94:5–6,7–8,9–10,14–15
Matthew 11:25–27

Thursday

JULY 18

• ST. CAMILLUS DE LELLIS, PRIEST •

Jesus said:
"Come to me, all you who labor and are burdened,
and I will give you rest."
—MATTHEW 11:28

For many of the people listening to Jesus, life was hard, poverty and struggle everyday realities. So, Jesus invites all who labor and are burdened, which would be most of his audience, to come to him and find rest. This is the intimate, comforting, and compassionate Jesus, who looks upon the people following him and feels nothing but love for them.

His invitation is remarkably straightforward. But it is an invitation Jesus continues to offer. Look up the next time you feel burdened; you will see Jesus gazing gently upon you and hear him quietly saying, "Come to me, and I will give you rest."

Isaiah 26:7–9,12,16–19
Psalm 102:13–14ab and 15,16–18,19–21
Matthew 11:28–30

> *When Hezekiah was mortally ill,*
> *the prophet Isaiah, son of Amoz, came and said to him:*
> *"Thus says the LORD: Put your house in order,*
> *for you are about to die; you shall not recover."*
> —ISAIAH 38:1

Scary words to hear: *Put your house in order.* Because I am of a certain age, I think a lot about putting my house in order. The truth is, most of us don't know when we will die; we just know that we will. Part of living a good life is preparing as best we can for a good death. I believe a good death involves making as many good choices as we can, from big, life-changing ones to small, seemingly inconsequential ones. Making good choices reduces our regrets, and those who die with the fewest regrets die the happiest.

Isaiah 38:1–6,21–22,7–8
Isaiah 38:10,11,12abcd,16
Matthew 12:1–8

Saturday
JULY 20

• ST. APOLLINARIUS, BISHOP AND MARTYR •

Why, O LORD, do you stand aloof?
Why hide in times of distress?
—PSALM 10:1

Even Jesus felt abandoned by God, so why shouldn't we feel
that way from time to time? But was Jesus abandoned by
God, or was his journey fraught with difficult decisions only
he could make because God had given him free will, as he
does all of us? What feels like God standing aloof might
actually be God allowing us the space to make important
choices. In our distress, we might not feel God's presence.
Perhaps God allows us to feel our distress so we can
recognize our need for him.

Micah 2:1–5
Psalm 10:1–2,3–4,7–8,14
Matthew 12:14–21

The apostles gathered together with Jesus
and reported all they had done and taught.
He said to them,
"Come away by yourselves to a deserted place and rest a while."
—MARK 6:30–31

Our days flash by in a blur of family responsibilities, work demands, and household duties. Some of us are on the go from the time we get out of bed until we return there at the end of a very long day. Like so much of what Jesus says in Scripture, it's not just for the audience he was speaking to at the time. His words have been preserved and passed on because they have meaning for us today. "Come and rest and be with me a while."

Jeremiah 23:1–6
Psalm 23:1–3,3–4,5,6 (1)
Ephesians 2:13–18
Mark 6:30–34

Monday

JULY 22

• ST. MARY MAGDALENE •

Mary stayed outside the tomb weeping.
And as she wept, she bent over into the tomb
and saw two angels in white sitting there,
one at the head and one at the feet
where the Body of Jesus had been.
And they said to her, "Woman, why are you weeping?"
—JOHN 20:11–13

Mary's weeping at the empty tomb of Jesus resonates through the ages for its palpable sense of her grieving. For Mary, the empty tomb is like Jesus dying a second time. She has lost even his lifeless body. But suddenly, Jesus is there, changed, unrecognizable at first, but alive. Imagine yourself beside Mary, sharing her whirlwind of emotions. What does it feel like to run back to the disciples, shouting, "He's alive! I have seen him!"

Song of Solomon 3:1–4b or 2 Corinthians 5:14–17
Psalm 63:2, 3–4,5–6,8–9
John 20:1–2, 11–18

Tuesday

JULY 23

• ST. BRIDGET OF SWEDEN, RELIGIOUS •

And stretching out his hand toward his disciples, he said,
"Here are my mother and my brothers.
For whoever does the will of my heavenly Father
is my brother, and sister, and mother."
—MATTHEW 12:49–50

While Mary and other family members are standing outside
where Jesus is speaking, Jesus tells the people inside with him
that *they* are his family. This appears incredibly insensitive,
and I don't know about you, but I am not about to insult
Mary. But shift perspective a little: he is telling the crowd
they are his family too, because they are listening to him and
following him. This should be of great comfort to us all; we
who follow Jesus and abide by his teachings are his family.
This is the radical inclusiveness of our God.

Micah 7:14–15,18–20
Psalm 85:2–4,5–6,7–8
Matthew 12:46–50

Wednesday

JULY 24

• ST. SHARBEL MAKHLŪF, PRIEST •

The word of the LORD came to me thus:

Before I formed you in the womb I knew you,
before you were born I dedicated you,
—JEREMIAH 1:5

We love to speculate about destiny, about what is predetermined or ordained for us. In our culture and time, we love to believe that we are in charge of our lives and our choices. That we become who we are through birth and family, education and society, time and training, relationships and realities. But what if the person we are was chosen by God long before we were conceived or born? What if God dedicated each of our lives for a unique purpose and plan? Wouldn't you want to know what the Lord created you to do? Ask him—it's not too late.

Jeremiah 1:1,4–10
Psalm 71:1–2,3–4a,5–6ab,15 and 17
Matthew 13:1–9

Thursday

JULY 25

*For we who live are constantly being given up to death
for the sake of Jesus,
so that the life of Jesus may be manifested in our mortal flesh.*
—2 CORINTHIANS 4:11

The internet is filled with collections of interesting messages
on church signs. Some are funny, some are deadly serious,
and some perhaps a little of both, like this one: "Be an organ
donor, give your heart to Jesus."

2 Corinthians 4:7–15
Psalm 126:1bc–2ab,2cd–3,4–5,6
Matthew 20:20–28

⋟ 236 ⋞

*[Jesus said,] "But the seed sown on rich soil
is the one who hears the word and understands it,
who indeed bears fruit and yields a hundred or sixty or thirtyfold."*
—MATTHEW 13:23

This week my wife and I went to the theater to watch a new documentary called *No Greater Love* on the life and ministry of St. Mother Teresa. It was inspiring and heartbreaking at the same time. She suffered such a long, dark night of the soul, but she never let it derail her calling. Before she ever became Mother Teresa, she was taught about our Lord by her mother and parish priests. They planted the seeds of faith early in her life, and in that rich soil she grew to become the saint who changed the world.

Jeremiah 3:14–17
Jeremiah 31:10,11–12abcd,13
Matthew 13:18–23

Saturday

JULY 27

My soul yearns and pines
for the courts of the LORD.
My heart and my flesh
cry out for the living God.
—PSALM 84:3

There is an incurable longing in our hearts, in our souls, and
in our bodies. It is a brokenness we feel, a sense of
displacement, a desire to return to a place we know but don't
really remember. We can spend our lives searching for
glimpses of this place. We do find tantalizing clues along the
way, flashes of familiar but fading memories. As we get older,
our yearning grows deeper. An urgency sets in; time may be
running out. What are we searching for, what are we longing
to rediscover? We are trying to find our way home. We are
simply homesick for heaven.

Jeremiah 7:1–11
Psalm 84:3,4,5–6a and 8a,11
Matthew 13:24–30

⇒ 238 ⇐

Brothers and sisters:
I, a prisoner for the Lord,
urge you to live in a manner worthy of the call you have received,
with all humility and gentleness, with patience,
bearing with one another through love.
—EPHESIANS 4:1–2

Paul's call to the followers of the Way in Ephesus remains as valid today as when he wrote in the specific time, location, and circumstance of his ministry. He urged that they/we live in a manner worthy of the call we have received. This is the call of the Lord, a call to completely change our values and our priorities. We are to live with gentleness, humility, and patience in this world. And most important, with love. Because wherever there is love, God is present.

2 Kings 4:42–44
Psalm 145:10–11,15–16,17–18
Ephesians 4:1–6
John 6:1–15

Monday

JULY 29

• ST. MARTHA •

Martha, burdened with much serving, came to him and said,
"Lord, do you not care
that my sister has left me by myself to do the serving?
Tell her to help me."
The Lord said to her in reply,
"Martha, Martha, you are anxious and worried about many things.
There is need of only one thing."
—LUKE 10:40–42

What is the "one thing" Jesus is talking about? If that "one thing" was important to Martha, then it is important to us, too. Perhaps "one thing" is our undivided attention to Jesus. We need to balance our daily business so we do not miss the moments in which we are called to be present, especially to our Lord.

Jeremiah 13:1–11 [Memorial: 1 John 4:7–16]
Deuteronomy 32:18–19,20,21 [Memorial: Ps 34:2–3,4–5,6–7,8–9,10–11]
John 11:19–27 or Luke 10:38–42

Tuesday

JULY 30

• ST. PETER CHRYSOLOGUS, BISHOP AND DOCTOR OF THE CHURCH •

"Then the righteous will shine like the sun
in the Kingdom of their Father."
—MATTHEW 13:43

There is a famous story and quote from Thomas Merton,
often referred to as the Fourth and Walnut Epiphany. It
happened in March of 1958, as Merton was walking around
the shopping district of downtown Louisville. After years of
feeling harsh condemnation toward many people in his life,
he had a revelation of pure love. He wrote, *"I was suddenly*
overwhelmed with the realization that I loved all those people, that they
were mine and I theirs. . . . If only everybody could realize this! But it
cannot be explained. There is no way of telling people that they are all
walking around shining like the sun."

Jeremiah 14:17–22
Psalm 79:8,9,11 and 13
Matthew 13:36–43

Wednesday

JULY 31

• ST. IGNATIUS OF LOYOLA, PRIEST •

For I am with you,
to deliver and rescue you, says the LORD.
—JEREMIAH 15:20B

Today the church celebrates the feast of St. Ignatius of Loyola. Among the prayers I say daily is one by Ignatius called the *suscipe*. It is a powerful prayer of gratitude and surrender.

Take, Lord, and receive all my liberty,
my memory, my understanding,
and my entire will,
all I have and call my own.
You have given all to me.
To you, Lord, I return it.
Everything is yours; do with it what you will.
Give me only your love and your grace,
that is enough for me.

Jeremiah 15:10,16–21
Psalm 59:2–3,4,10–11,17,18
Matthew 13:44–46

AUGUST 1

• ST. ALPHONSUS LIGUORI, BISHOP AND DOCTOR OF THE CHURCH •

Jesus said to his disciples:
"The Kingdom of heaven is like a net thrown into the sea,
which collects fish of every kind.
When it is full they haul it ashore
and sit down to put what is good into buckets.
What is bad they throw away."
—MATTHEW 13:47–48

This would have been a familiar scene for the people in the
time of Jesus. Watching the fishermen work, sorting the
good fish into buckets and the bad into other buckets. For a
parable, it is pretty straightforward. Later Jesus mentions
that, at the end of time, angels will come and sort the wicked
from the righteous, like the fishermen in the parable. But the
wicked will not simply get tossed into the bad buckets; they
will be consigned to the fiery furnace. High on my bucket
list is getting sorted into the right bucket!

Jeremiah 18:1–6
Psalm 146:1b–2,3–4,5–6ab
Matthew 13:47–53

Friday

AUGUST 2

• ST. EUSEBIUS OF VERCELLI, BISHOP • ST. PETER JULIAN EYMARD, PRIEST •

*In your great kindness answer me
with your constant help.*
—PSALM 69:14

Fr. Ben was in his car leaving a crowded parking lot when one of the lot attendants, seeing Ben's Roman collar, told him that he did not think he could go on living, and he asked Ben what he should do. Fr. Ben looked in his rearview mirror, saw the long line of impatient drivers behind him, turned to the young man, and said, "Think about what you love, think about the gifts God has given you, and ask God what he wants you to do next with those gifts. God will guide you." Then he blessed the young man and drove away.

Jeremiah 26:1–9
Psalm 69:5,8–10,14
Matthew 13:54–58

AUGUST 3

Prompted by her mother, she said,
"Give me here on a platter the head of John the Baptist."
The king was distressed,
but because of his oaths and the guests who were present,
he ordered that it be given, and he had John beheaded in the prison.
—MATTHEW 14:8–10

One of the things I love about Scripture is the unvarnished portrayal of terrible people who make terrible decisions for terrible reasons. Among them, Herod, and his decision to behead John the Baptist to please his scandalous bride and her daughter. As for lessons to be learned from this story, I'm not sure. Never make a decision in the heat of the moment? Maybe. But somewhere, languishing and second guessing himself still, I believe Herod is wringing his hands and wishing he could have that one back.

Jeremiah 26:11–16,24
Psalm 69:15–16,30–31,33–34
Matthew 14:1–12

Sunday

AUGUST 4

Brothers and sisters:
I declare and testify in the Lord
that you must no longer live as the Gentiles do,
in the futility of their minds;
—EPHESIANS 4:17

It's a curious phrase St. Paul uses: "in the futility of their minds." Paul believed that Jesus changed everything for everybody. The old ways of doing and being were futile. A believer needed to invite Jesus into his or her life and open up to the guidance of the Holy Spirit. Then a new self would replace the old self. Literally, we are to "take on Christ" and become new creations, and it is not something we can think our way into; it happens when we put our faith into action by following Jesus.

Exodus 16:2–4,12–15
Psalm 78:3–4,23–24,25,54 (24b)
Ephesians 4:17,20–24
John 6:24–35

Monday

AUGUST 5

• THE DEDICATION OF THE BASILICA OF ST. MARY MAJOR •

Taking the five loaves and the two fish, and looking up to heaven,
he said the blessing, broke the loaves,
and gave them to the disciples,
who in turn gave them to the crowds.
—MATTHEW 14:19

The miracle of the loaves and fishes appears in all four Gospels, suggesting its importance in the formation and teachings of the early church. The connection to our modern Liturgy of the Eucharist also attests to the ongoing primacy of this story. The message of this story is that Jesus can feed all who hunger. The appearance of limited provisions is not a hindrance to the Lord; all who seek him will be fed.

Jeremiah 28:1–17
Psalm 119:29,43,79,80,95,102
Matthew 14:13–21

⇒ 247 ⇐

Tuesday

AUGUST 6

• THE TRANSFIGURATION OF THE LORD •

You will do well to be attentive to it,
as to a lamp shining in a dark place,
until day dawns and the morning star rises in your hearts.
—2 PETER 1:19

The Transfiguration occurred after Jesus had told the apostles
that he would soon go to Jerusalem, where he would be
killed. This news caused panic among them. Knowing their
hearts were troubled, Jesus brought Peter, James, and John to
a high mountain. There they witnessed Jesus being
"transfigured" into a dazzling figure of light, and they saw
Moses and Elijah with him and heard the voice of God the
Father. It was Jesus who was transfigured, but it was the
apostles who were transformed, and Jesus knew that
transformed people transform others.

Daniel 7:9–10,13–14
Psalm 97:1–2,5–6,9
2 Peter 1:16–19
Mark 9:2–10

> *Then Jesus said to her in reply,*
> *"O woman, great is your faith!*
> *Let it be done for you as you wish."*
> *And her daughter was healed from that hour.*
> —MATTHEW 15:28

Jesus rebuffs the Canaanite woman rather rudely several
times, very uncharacteristic of him. But the Canaanite
woman, God bless her, does not let the disciples send her
away and does not let Jesus dissuade her. She knows Jesus
can heal her daughter, and she is not about to take no for an
answer. She persists until Jesus relents. He finally
acknowledges her great faith, and her daughter is healed.
The takeaway here is that it is okay to persist with Jesus, to
fight for his attention. Let your faith make you audacious,
because a miracle may hang in the balance.

Jeremiah 31:1–7
Jeremiah 31:10,11–12ab,13
Matthew 15:21–28

Thursday

AUGUST 8

• ST. DOMINIC, PRIEST •

Give me back the joy of your salvation,
and a willing spirit sustain in me.
—PSALM 51:14

This life is so brief, and we are all broken, a little lost, and deeply flawed. But there is a loving God who offers us salvation, joy, and the strength of spirit to endure all that life throws at us. All we need to do is ask. Ask the Lord for what you need. None of us is perfect; we are all human beings in the process of learning to be human, with God's help. To God, we are rare and beautiful creatures, wonderful in his eyes. Find joy, and you will find God.

Jeremiah 31:31–34
Psalm 51:12–13,14–15,18–19
Matthew 16:13–23

Friday

AUGUST 9

See, upon the mountains there advances
the bearer of good news,
announcing peace!
—NAHUM 2:1

We can be bearers of good news even when there seems to be nothing but a preponderance of bad news. We can announce peace and share it with others rather than spread unnecessary discord. We can choose to act with love in our hearts, even when we are frightened or overwhelmed. We can do all this because there is a spirit of God residing in each one of us and we can choose to let that spirit shine and illuminate the seemingly dark world. Be a bearer of good news and bring the peace of God wherever you go.

Nahum 2:1,3; 3:1–3,6–7
Deuteronomy 32:35cd–36ab,39abcd,41
Matthew 16:24–28

Brothers and sisters:
Whoever sows sparingly will also reap sparingly,
and whoever sows bountifully will also reap bountifully.
Each must do as already determined, without sadness or compulsion,
for God loves a cheerful giver.
Moreover, God is able to make every grace abundant for you,
so that in all things, always having all you need,
you may have an abundance for every good work.
—2 CORINTHIANS 9:6–8

There is no place in the world for gloomy Christians. The truth is, as Paul writes, we must find it in our hearts to give generously, to give joyfully. We will always have what we need because God has blessed each one of us abundantly. He in turn wants us to do the same, and cheerfully.

2 Corinthians 9:6–10
Psalm 112:1–2,5–6,7–8,9
John 12:24–26

Sunday

AUGUST 11

• NINETEENTH SUNDAY IN ORDINARY TIME •

Brothers and sisters: . . .
All bitterness, fury, anger, shouting, and reviling
must be removed from you, along with all malice.
And be kind to one another, compassionate,
forgiving one another as God has forgiven you in Christ.
—EPHESIANS 4:31–32

Paul states three characteristics of a Christian: being kind, being compassionate, and always forgiving. We are new creations in Christ, and as God has forgiven us in Christ, we must do the same with others. There is no gray area here for Paul. We must be kind to all. We must be compassionate in all our dealings with people. And we must be willing to forgive, no matter what, and always. Left to ourselves, this might prove impossible, but with Christ, it is possible.

1 Kings 19:4–8
Psalm 34:2–3,4–5,6–7,8–9 (9a)
Ephesians 4:30—5:2
John 6:41–51

AUGUST 12

Praise the LORD from the heavens;
praise him in the heights;
Praise him, all you his angels;
praise him, all you his hosts.
—PSALM 148:1–2

Today the church celebrates the feast day of St. Jane Frances
de Chantal, a remarkable French woman who lived in the
seventeenth century. A baroness, then a widow, finally a nun,
Jane's spiritual mentor was the great saint and writer St.
Francis de Sales, who was also a family friend. Jane was
canonized a century after her death. Passionate about prayer,
she wrote, "In prayer, more is accomplished by listening than
by talking."

Ezekiel 1:2–5,24–28c
Psalm 148:1–2,11–12,13,14
Matthew 17:22–27

Your decrees are my inheritance forever;
the joy of my heart they are.
—PSALM 119:111

This morning there is a beautiful sunrise, and a gentle breeze greets me on the front porch as I sit with my coffee and listen to birdsong in the surrounding trees. Spring blossoms wink everywhere in vivid color, like an artist's palette. The early morning sky turns azure blue. Later, it is evening. I am back on the porch, the sky spectacular in reds, oranges, and purples. The clouds shape-shifting dreams. I consider the gift of this day as the sun sets. Where was God today? Everywhere!

Ezekiel 2:8—3:4
Psalm 119:14,24,72,103,111,131
Matthew 18:1–5,10,12–14

Wednesday

AUGUST 14

• ST. MAXIMILIAN MARIA KOLBE, PRIEST AND MARTYR •

Praise, you servants of the LORD,
praise the name of the LORD.
—PSALM 113:1

Today we honor Maximilian Kolbe, a Polish Catholic priest
and Franciscan friar. He died in the notorious WWII
concentration camp Auschwitz. After a full life, with many
accomplishments, he volunteered to take the place of a
prisoner chosen by the Nazis to be executed by starvation.
Eventually, Kolbe was killed by a lethal injection of carbolic
acid. The man Kolbe saved survived WWII and was present
for Kolbe's canonization by John Paul II in 1986.

Ezekiel 9:1–7; 10:18–22
Psalm 113:1–2,3–4,5–6
Matthew 18:15–20

AUGUST 15

• THE ASSUMPTION OF THE BLESSED VIRGIN MARY •

For since death came through man,
the resurrection of the dead came also through man.
For just as in Adam all die,
so too in Christ shall all be brought to life.
—1 CORINTHIANS 15:21–22

Since 1950, the church has taught the doctrine of Mary's bodily assumption into heaven. She was spared the usual death, and the church teaches that her physical body was joined with her immortal soul in heaven. Her arrival must have been the cause of one great, momentous celebration. Every soul in heaven overjoyed to welcome her home.

<table>
<tr><td align="center">VIGIL:</td><td align="center">DAY:</td></tr>
<tr><td align="center">1 Chronicles 15:3–4,15–16; 16:1–2</td><td align="center">Revelation 11:19a; 12:1–6a,10ab</td></tr>
<tr><td align="center">Psalm 132:6–7,9–10,13–14</td><td align="center">Psalm 45:10,11,12,16</td></tr>
<tr><td align="center">1 Corinthians 15:54b–57</td><td align="center">1 Corinthians 15:20–27</td></tr>
<tr><td align="center">Luke 11:27–28</td><td align="center">Luke 1:39–56</td></tr>
</table>

Friday

AUGUST 16

• ST. STEPHEN OF HUNGARY •

God indeed is my savior;
I am confident and unafraid.
My strength and my courage is the LORD,
and he has been my savior.

—ISAIAH 12:2

How many of us have the courage to live unafraid or have the strength of our convictions and the confidence to act upon them? It is not easy to do. Today, the Church honors St. Stephen of Hungary, born in the tumultuous era at the end of the first millennium. Born a pagan into a violent and cruel time in what is now modern Hungary, Stephen, with strength and courage, brought order and peace to his world through his conversion to Christianity and devotion to the Church.

Ezekiel 16:1–15,60,63 or Ezekiel 16:59–63
Isaiah 12:2–3,4bcd,5–6
Matthew 19:3–12

AUGUST 17

*[Jesus said,] "Let the children come to me, and do not prevent them;
for the Kingdom of heaven belongs to such as these."*
—MATTHEW 19:14–15

Jesus loved and protected little children; he said they
belonged to the kingdom of heaven. I am reminded of the
story of a little girl who wanted time alone with the infant
brother her parents had just brought home from the hospital.
Her parents were suspicious she might harm the baby. But
the big sister was persistent, and eventually her parents
decided to allow her ten minutes alone with her baby brother
in his room. After they closed the door, they listened quietly
to the baby monitor. They began to cry when they heard
their daughter say, "Baby brother, tell me what heaven is like.
I'm starting to forget."

Ezekiel 18:1–10,13b,30–32
Psalm 51:12–13,14–15,18–19
Matthew 19:13–15

Forsake foolishness that you may live;
advance in the way of understanding.
—PROVERBS 9:6

Thomas Aquinas is one of the towering intellectuals of the church, his contributions to Western thought so substantial they have influenced philosophy and theology for eight centuries. Toward the end of his life, the great man who had reconciled Aristotelian logic to Christian theology began to have mystical experiences that blew up much of his worldview. He said to a friend: "I have seen things that make all my writings seem like straw." At its heart, the experience of God is beyond words. It is foolishness to think that God can be described. This is the beginning of understanding.

Proverbs 9:1–6
Psalm 34:2–3,4–5,6–7
Ephesians 5:15–20
John 6:51–58

Monday

AUGUST 19

• ST. JOHN EUDES, PRIEST •

You forgot the God who gave you birth.
—DEUTERONOMY 32:18

It can be easy to forget we were created out of love to love
and be loved, especially if the circumstances of our lives are
difficult. But we can reconcile ourselves to the fact that we
are children of a loving God who created us to share the joy
of his creation with him and others. As children of God, we
have an enormous responsibility to share the love that is the
source of our creation. Do not forget that in God's eyes, we
are all precious, and our birthright is to be loved.

Ezekiel 24:15–23
Deuteronomy 32:18–19,20,21
Matthew 19:16–22

⇒ 261 ⇐

Tuesday

AUGUST 20

• ST. BERNARD, ABBOT AND DOCTOR OF THE CHURCH •

Jesus looked at them and said,
"For men this is impossible,
but for God all things are possible."
—MATTHEW 19:25–26

This comes after Jesus tells the disciples how hard it is for a rich person to enter the kingdom of heaven. However good the wealthy have it on earth, they may not have those same advantages in the next life. Heaven is governed by a different set of rules. That does not mean it is better to be poor but that, for someone with seemingly everything, it's not easy to give it all up and follow Jesus. Wealth can be a distraction to the Good News, and we do not want to be so distracted that we miss Christ's heavenly invitation.

Ezekiel 28:1–10
Deuteronomy 32:26–27ab,27cd–28,30,35cd–36ab
Matthew 19:23–30

AUGUST 21

• ST. PIUS X, POPE •

[Jesus said,] "Are you envious because I am generous?"
Thus, the last will be first, and the first will be last.
—MATTHEW 20:15B–6

The story of the landowner and the laborers helps us
understand that it does not matter to God when we show up,
only *that* we show up. God operates out of endless and
unlimited generosity. For those who view the world as a
meritocracy, this can be challenging. But as recipients of
God's undeserved, unearned generosity, we should be grateful
that God's only condition is that we say yes to his invitation.

Ezekiel 34:1–11
Psalm 23:1–3a,3b–4,5,6
Matthew 20:1–16

Thursday

AUGUST 22

[Jesus said,] "Many are invited, but few are chosen."
—MATTHEW 22:14

Jesus offers this aphoristic observation at the end of telling
the parable about the king who threw a wedding feast for his
son, with few guests showing up and some inappropriately
attired for the formal event. Jesus tells this to the community
around him, who neither recognizes him as the king's son or
realizes the universality of his Father's invitation. The
wedding feast is the kingdom of God, a celebration to which
everyone is invited, though most ignore the invitation, while
others are unprepared for it. What is interesting is the
phrasing "few are chosen" rather than "few choose to attend."
God invites, God chooses, but our part is to
accept and attend.

Ezekiel 36:23–28
Psalm 51:12–13,14–15,18–19
Matthew 22:1–14

AUGUST 23

• ST. ROSE OF LIMA, VIRGIN •

"Teacher, which commandment in the law is the greatest?"
[Jesus] said to him,
"You shall love the Lord, your God, with all your heart,
with all your soul, and with all your mind.
This is the greatest and the first commandment."
—MATTHEW 22:36–38

Seeking to test Jesus, the Pharisees ask him which is the
greatest commandment. Jesus answers clearly and
definitively: Love God with everything you have, everything
you are. Love fiercely, love completely. Here is the message
at the heart of the Good News: we are here to love. Jesus
adds that we are also to love our neighbors as we love
ourselves. Then he finishes by telling his audience that
everything important to them depends on these two
commandments: love God, love one another.

Ezekiel 37:1–14
Psalm 107:2–3,4–5,6–7,8–9
Matthew 22:34–40

Saturday

AUGUST 24

• ST. BARTHOLOMEW, APOSTLE •

Let all your works give you thanks, O LORD,
and let your faithful ones bless you.
—PSALM 145:10

It is important not to forget that, while we are continually
blessed by the works of God, we in turn show our gratitude
for the Lord's works by blessing him.

Revelation 21:9b–14
Psalm 145:10–11,12–13,17–18
John 1:45–51

And [Jesus] said,
"For this reason I have told you that no one can come to me
unless it is granted him by my Father."
As a result of this,
many of his disciples returned to their former way of life
and no longer accompanied him.
—JOHN 6:65–66

The next time you get down on yourself for not being as
faithful as you want to be, think about this: disciples who
were with Jesus, who saw him perform miracles, who heard
his teachings, could turn their backs on him and return to
their old ways of life because they found the path too
difficult. So be kind to yourself. It is hard following Jesus, but
stay the course, keep the faith.

Joshua 24:1–2a,15–17,18b
Psalm 34:2–3,16–17,18–19,20–21 (9a)
Ephesians 5:21–32 or 5:2a,25–32
John 6:60–69

*[Jesus said,] "Woe to you, scribes and Pharisees, you hypocrites.
You lock the Kingdom of heaven before men.
You do not enter yourselves,
nor do you allow entrance to those trying to enter."*
—MATTHEW 23:13–14

Jesus reserves some of his greatest ire for those who are in
positions of spiritual authority, leaders who do not lead
people to the kingdom but effectively block the way for
others and do not enter themselves. We may at first read this
as referring in our time to the leadership of the church. But
all who are baptized, including the laity, are part of the
spiritual priesthood of the church, and therefore it is upon all
of us to lead, to welcome, and to make way for all who want
to enter the kingdom.

2 Thessalonians 1:1–5,11–12
Psalm 96:1–2a,2b–3,4–5
Matthew 23:13–22

Tuesday

AUGUST 27

• ST. MONICA •

May our Lord Jesus Christ himself and God our Father,
who has loved us and given us everlasting encouragement
and good hope through his grace,
encourage your hearts and strengthen them
in every good deed and word.
—2 THESSALONIANS 2:16–17

Paul wrote this note of encouragement to the community of
believers in Thessalonica around AD 50. Within the early
communities there was a palpable anticipation of Jesus'
imminent return. But Paul began to rethink Jesus' return—not
the *if* but the *when*. So, he began to give form and structure to
the lives of the early faithful, for if they had to wait, he
wanted them to know that they had everything they needed.
Paul showed the early church, and us, how to live in the
tension between the "already" and the "not yet."

2 Thessalonians 2:1–3a,14–17
Psalm 96:10,11–12,13
Matthew 23:23–26

AUGUST 28

• ST. AUGUSTINE, BISHOP AND DOCTOR OF THE CHURCH •

Blessed are you who fear the LORD,
who walk in his ways!
—PSALM 128:1

St. Augustine lived sixteen hundred years ago, but if he were alive today, he might be the pope. He certainly would be one of the best-selling spiritual writers of our time. Oprah would select him for her book club. He would be a social-media star and have the most popular podcast on Apple, and you might have a poster or be wearing a T-shirt with quotes attributed to him: "There is no saint without a past, no sinner without a future." "The measure of love is to love without measuring." "Pray as though everything depended on God. Work as though everything depended on you."

2 Thessalonians 3:6–10,16–18
Psalm 128:1–2,4–5
Matthew 23:27–32

Thursday

AUGUST 29

He will keep you firm to the end,
irreproachable on the day of our Lord Jesus Christ.
—1 CORINTHIANS 1:8

Paul writes to the faithful in Corinth, reminding them that
Christ will keep his promise and provide his grace until the
very end of time, the day of the Lord—not because we have
earned it through our good works and our devotion but
because God is good and devoted and keeps his promises.
God's love for us is steadfast and strong, as much on the last
day as it was on the first. Such are the promises of God.

1 Corinthians 1:1–9
Psalm 145:2–3,4–5,6–7
Mark 6:17–29 [Matthew 24:42–51] [The Mark passage is from the Memorial readings.]

*For the foolishness of God is wiser than human wisdom,
and the weakness of God is stronger than human strength.*
—1 CORINTHIANS 1:25

For cultures such as those of the ancient Greeks and Romans,
who worshipped strength and overt acts of physical power, a
god who willingly died a criminal's death on a Roman cross
was both a stumbling block philosophically and an
incomprehensible leap of faith. Paul flips the script of the
ancient world by pointing out that Jesus overcame death,
that the cross, a symbol of Roman terror and domination, has
now become a sign of God's power over fear and death. That
the old world has been forever changed by one perfect
sacrifice. From apparent weakness has come strength, and
from seeming foolishness, divine wisdom. A new world, a
new king, Christ among us.

1 Corinthians 1:17–25
Psalm 33:1–2,4–5,10–11
Matthew 25:1–13

AUGUST 31

For to everyone who has,
more will be given and he will grow rich;
but from the one who has not,
even what he has will be taken away.
—MATTHEW 25:29

The above Scripture passage is from the parable of the talents. It is simple, really: All of us have been given gifts. These gifts are to be used to make things better, to be helpful, to do our work in the world. If we do this, we will multiply our gifts, find meaning and purpose, and make the world a little better than we found it. That is the good news. The bad news is that if we do not use the gifts we have been given, we will lose those gifts, and worse. Life Step #1: discover your gifts. Life Step #2: start using them.

1 Corinthians 1:26–31
Psalm 33:12–13,18–19,20–21
Matthew 25:14–30

Be doers of the word and not hearers only, deluding yourselves.
—JAMES 1:22

Faith requires action. Listening to the word of God makes life worth living and brings the truth home to our hearts. But that truth also brings the realization that none of us will be saved until all of us are saved. Following Christ is about connecting with others, sharing the Good News. Let us not romanticize faith's responsibilities. If following Christ is following a truth worth living for, it is also following a truth worth dying for. This is what James is saying: We must be doers of the word, not merely hearers of the word. This is where true transformation of souls takes place.

Deuteronomy 4:1–2,6–8
Psalm 15:2–3,3–4,4–5 (1a)
James 1:17–18,21b–22,27
Mark 7:1–8,14–15,21–23

*For I resolved to know nothing while I was with you
except Jesus Christ, and him crucified.*
—1 CORINTHIANS 2:2

Speakers and orators in Paul's day used a lot of razzle-dazzle
to impress their audiences. Paul reminds the Corinthians that
when he first came to them, he did none of this. What's
worth noting is that Paul was an educated, well-traveled,
effective debater with great speaking chops. He knew lots of
the tricks of the preaching trade, but he chose not to use any
of them. Rather, in humility, trusting the simple message of
Christ crucified, he witnessed to the efficacy of the cross.
Paul put Christ crucified front and center and let the message
speak for itself. As followers of Christ, let us not forget that it
is about the message, not the messengers.

1 Corinthians 2:1–5
Psalm 119:97,98,99,100,101,102
Luke 4:16–30

*They were all amazed and said to one another,
"What is there about his word?"*
—LUKE 4:36

Jesus has just cast out an unclean spirit while speaking and teaching in the synagogue in Capernaum. This is early in his ministry. Luke says of the crowd, "They were astonished at his teaching because he spoke with authority." Not only did Jesus command the crowd with his learned discourse on the Scriptures but also with his ability to cast out demons. Luke puts an interesting choice of words into the mouths of those hearing and watching Jesus: "What is there about his word?" Jesus *is* the Word. The Word was with God and the Word was God. Yes, there certainly was something about his word!

1 Corinthians 2:10b–16
Psalm 145:8–9,10–11,12–13ab,13cd–14
Luke 4:31–37

Therefore, neither the one who plants nor the one who waters is anything,
but only God, who causes the growth.
—1 CORINTHIANS 3:7

Paul is offering the Corinthians of his day, and those in the church of our day, an important lesson. All God's ministers and people have their roles to play, their work to do, in building the kingdom of God. But ultimately it is God who does the work through us and our efforts. None of us is more important than any of us. This community of the faithful is not a meritocracy but a community of grace. It operates on the unearned grace of a loving God who requires only that we allow the grace to produce like a healthy farmer's field or a beautiful garden.

1 Corinthians 3:1–9
Psalm 33:12–13,14–15,20–21
Luke 4:38–44

SEPTEMBER 5

Who can ascend the mountain of the LORD?
or who can stand in his holy place?
—PSALM 24:3

The simple answer to the psalmist's question is, none of us.
But with a righteous and clean heart, we can attempt to
ascend the mountain of the Lord. And with a humble and
reverent spirit we can seek to stand in the Lord's holy place.
We may find that the journey is not what we expected, for
we arrive not by effort but by grace. It is not a journey to a
distant destination. For the holy mountain of the Lord, this
holy place of the psalmist, is found within each of us. It is a
journey within, to discover the God who created us in love,
and it is the most important journey of our lives.

1 Corinthians 3:18–23
Psalm 24:1bc–2,3–4ab,5–6
Luke 5:1–11

SEPTEMBER 6

Therefore, do not make any judgment before the appointed time,
until the Lord comes,
for he will bring to light what is hidden in darkness
and will manifest the motives of our hearts,
and then everyone will receive praise from God.
—1 CORINTHIANS 4:5

We are not called to judge one another, because we do not
know what is hidden in others' hearts. Only the Lord knows
what is in our hearts, and he will be the judge when he
comes again at the appointed time. Only then will the
darkness be made light, secrets be revealed, motives be
understood. Until then, our work is to share our gifts, to help
one another, and to build the kingdom of God. For now, it is
enough that we wait in joyful hope for the Lord's return.

1 Corinthians 4:1–5
Psalm 37:3–4,5–6,27–28,39–40
Luke 5:33–39

SEPTEMBER 7

The LORD is near to all who call upon him,
to all who call upon him in truth.
—PSALM 145:18

Everything in the world is governed by either love or fear. Love enlivens us, opens us to one another, connects and expands us. Fear shuts us down, closes us off from one another, makes us small. Love is the language of the Lord gently calling to you. Fear is the voice of the enemy, causing you distress and anxiety. Whom will you listen for? Whom will you call upon?

1 Corinthians 4:6b–15
Psalm 145:17–18,19–20,21
Luke 6:1–5

Say to those whose hearts are frightened:
Be strong, fear not!
Here is your God,
he comes with vindication;
with divine recompense
he comes to save you.
—ISAIAH 35:4

Repetition is the first and most powerful skill of education. Teaching by way of repetition turns a heard statement into a learned skill. The best teachers use repetition strategically and to great effect. So, it should be no surprise to hear certain themes repeated frequently throughout Scripture, such as "Be strong. Do not fear!" This is almost always followed by the promise of God to be with us, to accompany us, to save us.

Isaiah 35:4–7a
Psalm 146:6–7,8–9,9–10 (1b)
James 2:1–5
Mark 7:31–37

SEPTEMBER 9

• ST. PETER CLAVER, PRIEST •

Then Jesus said to them,
"I ask you, is it lawful to do good on the sabbath
rather than to do evil,
to save life rather than to destroy it?"
—LUKE 6:9

Upon a close reading of Scripture, we see how many times
Jesus ends up in disputes with the religious authorities. So
many of his teachings are challenged by the Pharisees, so
many of his healings are questioned by the scribes. And yet,
Jesus persists. It is as if he is on a collision course with the
power structure. How is it that a man who preached pure
love, forgiveness, and peace could be such a threat? When
Jesus comes again, will we make the same mistakes? Or will
we understand this time that love is truly greater than
the law?

1 Corinthians 5:1–8
Psalm 5:5–6,7,12
Luke 6:6–11

SEPTEMBER 10

*Everyone in the crowd sought to touch him
because power came forth from him and healed them all.*
—LUKE 6:19

What an extraordinary statement! Scripture is filled with
them, and it is easy to blow right by them in our reading.
That is why encountering Jesus in the Scriptures by slowing
down with Lectio Divina and imaginative prayer, immersing
ourselves in these incredible stories, can powerfully connect
us to the Gospels in an entirely different way. Try to imagine
the crowds surging around Jesus, grabbing on to him,
reaching out to touch him. Some desperate, some suffering
for years, some hopeful, some doubtful, but all taking the
chance, hoping to be healed. And what does Luke say? The
crowd could feel his power, and he healed them all. Our God
is an amazing God.

1 Corinthians 6:1–11
Psalm 149:1b–2,3–4,5–6a and 9b
Luke 6:12–19

SEPTEMBER 11

Raising his eyes toward his disciples Jesus said:

*"Blessed are you who are poor,
for the Kingdom of God is yours."*
—LUKE 6:20

What does Jesus mean in this passage when he speaks of the "poor"? Is he speaking about economic hardship? Or is he speaking about a condition of being excluded or left out of the mainstream for any number of reasons, such as lack of connection, feelings of isolation, loss of meaning, or perhaps mental or physical challenges? He may be telling us that when we know the poverty of a life without something essential, we can also imagine life without God. The gospel sounds different when we are broken and hungry. The "poverty" of this world becomes the door by which we enter the next world, the kingdom of God.

1 Corinthians 7:25–31
Psalm 45:11–12,14–15,16–17
Luke 6:20–26

SEPTEMBER 12

*[Jesus said,] "For the measure with which you measure
will in return be measured out to you."*
—LUKE 6:38B

Jesus has just delivered one of his most stunning series of
teachings before ending with this quotable summation. His
message is essentially the Golden Rule. At the heart of most
spiritual traditions, there is this core underlying truth.
Christianity, Judaism, Hinduism, Islam, and Buddhism all
teach that what we offer the world will be returned to us in
kind. If we were to take nothing else from the teachings of
Jesus but were to apply and live by this one operative truth,
we would reshape how we approach everything in life—and
in death.

1 Corinthians 8:1b–7,11–13
Psalm 139:1b–3,13–14ab,23–24
Luke 6:27–38

SEPTEMBER 13

Why do you notice the splinter in your brother's eye,
but do not perceive the wooden beam in your own?
How can you say to your brother,
"Brother, let me remove that splinter in your eye,"
when you do not even notice the wooden beam in your own eye?
You hypocrite! Remove the wooden beam from your eye first;
then you will see clearly
to remove the splinter in your brother's eye.
—LUKE 6:41–42

Two things are going on in Jesus' teaching here: first is a
condition, and second is an action. The condition is our lack
of awareness, which is our big problem. The action is taking
care of our own big problem first, which then allows us to
see clearly and help others.

1 Corinthians 9:16–19,22b–27
Psalm 84:3,4,5–6,12
Luke 6:39–42

SEPTEMBER 14

• THE EXALTATION OF THE HOLY CROSS •

Because of this, God greatly exalted him
and bestowed on him the name
that is above every name,
that at the name of Jesus
every knee should bend,
of those in heaven and on earth and under the earth,
and every tongue confess that
Jesus Christ is Lord,
to the glory of God the Father.
—PHILIPPIANS 2:9–11

My mother was a devout, prayerful person. When I became
serious about my faith, she was delighted. She would often
tell me that all I needed to do was call upon the name of
Jesus. She believed the name of Jesus was both the shortest
and most powerful prayer we could pray. I've been surprised
by how much wiser my mother became as I got older.

Numbers 21:4b–9
Psalm 78:1bc–2,34–35,36–37,38
Philippians 2:6–11
John 3:13–17

The Lord GOD opens my ear that I may hear;
and I have not rebelled,
have not turned back.
—ISAIAH 50:5

When God opens our ears—and our hearts—we are never again the people we were. And upon being called by God, we must accept one of the oldest truths of self-discovery: the only way forward is through whatever we find ourselves in. There is no going back, there is no turning away. Faith calls us forward; the Lord beckons us with strength for the journey and salvation as our destination. We must stay the course, keep the faith, and finish the race. He will be with us every step of the way, no matter how hard things get. The way forward is through.

Isaiah 50:5–9a
Psalm 116:1–2,3–4,5–6,8–9 (9)
James 2:14–18
Mark 8:27–35

SEPTEMBER 16

• ST. CORNELIUS, POPE, AND ST. CYPRIAN, BISHOP, MARTYRS •

For I received from the Lord what I also handed on to you,
that the Lord Jesus, on the night he was handed over,
took bread and, after he had given thanks,
broke it and said, "This is my Body that is for you.
Do this in remembrance of me."
—1 CORINTHIANS 11:23-24

Paul understood deeply that what Jesus did at the Last
Supper was central to the growing faith, and he knew
continuing it was more than simple ritual remembrance. The
word *anamnesis* comes closest to explaining what happens
during the Liturgy of the Eucharist at Mass. We are not just
recalling the Last Supper but are stepping into the past with
Jesus at the Last Supper. We are connecting the living past to
the present moment through sacramental grace.

1 Corinthians 11:17–26,33
Psalm 40:7–8a,8b–9,10,17
Luke 7:1–10

Know that the LORD is God;
he made us, his we are.
—PSALM 100:3A

Another school shooting this week. A stray bullet killed a seven-year-old in the city. Another report in the news of a death by road rage. A story of parents charged with killing their baby. What do these random acts of horrific violence have in common? Who can say for sure, but I do believe that, if the perpetrators knew the Lord, if they knew God loved them, and if they believed that they were God's loving creations, things might have been different. Call me naive, but I cannot imagine that the world would suffer so much anguish and needless violence if people knew that God loved them.

1 Corinthians 12:12–14,27–31a
Psalm 100:1b–2,3,4,5
Luke 7:11–17

SEPTEMBER 18

Strive eagerly for the greatest spiritual gifts.

But I shall show you a still more excellent way.
—1 CORINTHIANS 12:31

In 2008, I took a deep dive into St. Paul. I read books, listened to audios, watched videos, anything I could do to understand Paul and his world. I investigated, and I got something out of everything I found. Paul is largely responsible for the Christianity we practice today. Without St. Paul, it is likely that Christianity would be a small Mediterranean sect within Judaism. The apostles wanted to keep the Way of Jesus within the Jewish faith. But Paul's view was more expansive, inclusive. Paul knew that Jesus had come for *everyone*. Paul's vision prevailed. Paul was like a finger pointing to the sun, and that sun was Jesus.

1 Corinthians 12:31—13:13
Psalm 33:2–3,4–5,12 and 22
Luke 7:31–35

SEPTEMBER 19

You are my God, and I give thanks to you;
O my God, I extol you.
—PSALM 118:28

Extol is an interesting word. We seldom use it except on occasion when we are "extolling someone's virtues." In other Scripture translations, *extol* might be exchanged with *glorify*, *praise*, or *honor*. We can also use *exalt* or *rejoice*, but you get the meaning. The psalmist is speaking about an enthusiastic, energetic appreciation of God. Not a quiet, prayerful "Thank you, Lord" but rather a jump-up, clap-your-hands, shout-it-from-the-rooftops kind of "THANK YOU, LORD!" When's the last time you felt the passion to extol the Lord that way?

1 Corinthians 15:1–11
Psalm 118:1b–2,16ab–17,28
Luke 7:36–50

SEPTEMBER 20

Jesus journeyed from one town and village to another,
preaching and proclaiming the good news of the Kingdom of God.
Accompanying him were the Twelve
and some women who had been cured of evil spirits and infirmities,
Mary, called Magdalene, from whom seven demons had gone out,
Joanna, the wife of Herod's steward Chuza,
Susanna, and many others
who provided for them out of their resources.
—LUKE 8:1–3

Luke points out that the early disciples were held together by a group of supportive and hardworking women. How important were these women? Well, one of them was the mother of our Lord; another was the first person the risen Lord appeared to.

1 Corinthians 15:12–20
Psalm 17:1bcd,6–7,8b and 15
Luke 8:1–3

SEPTEMBER 21

• ST. MATTHEW, APOSTLE AND EVANGELIST •

[Jesus said,] "Go and learn the meaning of the words,
I desire mercy, not sacrifice.
I did not come to call the righteous but sinners."
—MATTHEW 9:13

Throughout the Old Testament, sacrifice was a primary form
of offering, which gained God's graces and blessings. Now, in
the Gospel of Matthew, we hear Jesus say that the age of
sacrifice is over and the age of mercy is beginning. Mercy
replaces sacrifice because Jesus himself became the perfect
sacrifice that rendered all other sacrifices unnecessary.

Ephesians 4:1–7,11–13
Psalm 19:2–3,4–5
Matthew 9:9–13

And the fruit of righteousness is sown in peace
for those who cultivate peace.
—JAMES 3:18

In Hebrew, the word for peace is *shalom*. Shalom does not mean what we think of as peace today—the absence of war and/or conflict. Shalom means "completeness, or wholeness, or fullness." We can find this kind of peace only when we stop striving and desiring and begin to accept that God has given us everything we need in this moment. In order to cultivate peace, we must become peaceful ourselves. Perhaps Martin Luther King Jr. said it best: "Be the peace you wish to see in the world."

Wisdom 2:12,17–20
Psalm 54:3–4,5,6 and 8 (6b)
James 3:16—4:3
Mark 9:30–37

SEPTEMBER 23

• ST. PIUS OF PIETRELCINA, PRIEST •

Refuse no one the good on which he has a claim
when it is in your power to do it for him.
—PROVERBS 3:27

If it is in your power to help someone, do it. Don't withhold your help; don't defer your help. If somebody needs something and you can provide it, choose to help. If all of us believed that we could get the help we needed, when we needed it, the world would be a much happier place.

Proverbs 3:27–34
Psalm 15:2–3a,3bc–4ab,5
Luke 8:16–18

SEPTEMBER 24

*Give me discernment, that I may observe your law
and keep it with all my heart.*
—PSALM 119:34

There is a higher law that calls us to live and love with
greater care and compassion for our brothers and sisters, and
that's God's law. We all make poor choices from time to time,
but through discernment and submitting to the will of God,
we can make more good choices than bad choices. From
good choices come good results. From poor choices come
poor results. You might find this overly simplistic, but think
about it: When we make good decisions, we invite God into
the process. We seek to align with God's will. We don't act in
our own self-interest. We consider the good of others. Isn't
that the heart of the gospel message?

Proverbs 21:1–6,10–13
Psalm 119:1,27,30,34,35,44
Luke 8:19–21

SEPTEMBER 25

Every word of God is tested;
he is a shield to those who take refuge in him.
—PROVERBS 30:5

Each day we give ourselves to God in trust, and each day we are transformed by that offering. When we trust in the word of God, he leads us, he guides us, shows us the way. When we take refuge in God, he protects us from within and without. To take refuge in God is to choose God. Choosing God is the act of giving ourselves over to God, and there is no greater gift, no greater or more glorious exchange. Every soul that opens to God brings that much more of God into our world. Choosing God changes the world and brings the kingdom of God a little closer.

Proverbs 30:5–9
Psalm 119:29,72,89,101,104,163
Luke 9:1–6

SEPTEMBER 26

• ST. COSMAS AND ST. DAMIAN, MARTYRS •

What has been, that will be;
what has been done, that will be done.
Nothing is new under the sun.
—ECCLESIASTES 1:9

It may be a pessimistic comfort to think that there is nothing new under the sun, but in a strange way, it's also a freeing notion. All the "woulda, coulda, shoulda" worrying about what you did, what you didn't do, what you said, what you should have said—in the scheme of things, none of it matters all that much. This is not an excuse for bad behavior; it's simply allowing for some necessary life perspective. So let go of some of what burdens you; you're not the first person to experience what you're experiencing, and you won't be the last. Find some peace in this.

Ecclesiastes 1:2–11
Psalm 90:3–4,5–6,12–13,14 and 17bc
Luke 9:7–9

Once when Jesus was praying in solitude,
and the disciples were with him,
he asked them, "Who do the crowds say that I am?"
—LUKE 9:18

Jesus asks this question three times in the Gospels. Eventually, all of us who follow him must answer the question for ourselves. Who do we say that Jesus is? Find a quiet moment, imagine yourself with Jesus, and imagine him asking you directly, "Who do you say that I am?" What will your answer be? If you want to know the state of your relationship with the Lord, your answer will be a pretty good indication.

Ecclesiastes 3:1–11
Psalm 144:1b and 2abc,3–4
Luke 9:18–22

SEPTEMBER 28

• ST. WENCESLAUS, MARTYR • ST. LAWRENCE RUIZ
AND COMPANIONS, MARTYRS •

Fill us at daybreak with your kindness,
that we may shout for joy and gladness all our days.
—PSALM 90:14

This morning, if you are feeling the slightest anxiety, if
you're not sure what the day has in store for you, pause for a
moment and consider the three most important things in life:
Choose to be kind. Choose to be kind. Choose to be kind.
By day's end, don't be surprised if joy and gladness fill
your heart.

Ecclesiastes 11:9—12:8
Psalm 90:3–4,5–6,12–13,14 and 17
Luke 9:43b–45

At that time, John said to Jesus,
"Teacher, we saw someone driving out demons in your name,
and we tried to prevent him because he does not follow us."
Jesus replied, "Do not prevent him.
There is no one who performs a mighty deed in my name
who can at the same time speak ill of me.
For whoever is not against us is for us."
—MARK 9:38–40

Jesus is telling the disciples that while he chose them, they are in fact not that special. Anyone who acts in the name of Jesus is capable of great works. All followers of Jesus are moving in the same direction. Those closest to Jesus, and those following from afar. The message is what counts, not proximity to the Messenger.

Numbers 11:25–29
Psalm 19:8,10,12–13,14 (9a)
James 5:1–6
Mark 9:38–43,45,47–48

⇒ 302 ⇐

Then Job began to tear his cloak and cut off his hair.
He cast himself prostrate upon the ground, and said,

"Naked I came forth from my mother's womb,
and naked shall I go back again.
The LORD gave and the LORD has taken away;
blessed be the name of the LORD!"

In all this Job did not sin,
nor did he say anything disrespectful of God.
—JOB 1:20–22

The book of Job is unique among the writings in Scripture; it
is an object lesson on how to find meaning in suffering. And
while most of the Bible tells the story of a God who never
gives up on his people, the book of Job tells the story of a
man who never gives up on his God.

Job 1:6–22
Psalm 17:1bcd,2–3,6–7
Luke 9:46–50

OCTOBER 1

• ST. THÉRÈSE OF THE CHILD JESUS, VIRGIN AND DOCTOR OF
THE CHURCH •

O LORD, my God, by day I cry out;
at night I clamor in your presence.
Let my prayer come before you;
incline your ear to my call for help.
—PSALM 88:2–3

Praying the Psalms is like praying from God's own prayer
book. When we pray the Psalms, we are echoing the very
words of David, Solomon, and Moses. We are also entering a
stream of uninterrupted worship more than three thousand
years old. In Psalm 90, attributed to Moses, we are
worshipping the God of Moses, literally the God of the
burning bush, of the parting of the Red Sea, and of the Ten
Commandments. Imagine that.

Job 3:1–3,11–17,20–23
Psalm 88:2–3,4–5,6,7–8
Luke 9:51–56

[Job said:]
God is wise in heart and mighty in strength;
who has withstood him and remained unscathed?

He removes the mountains before they know it;
he overturns them in his anger.
He shakes the earth out of its place,
and the pillars beneath it tremble.
He commands the sun, and it rises not;
he seals up the stars.
—JOB 9:4–7

In addition to helping us find meaning in suffering, the book of Job also offers us a valuable lesson: the incredible scale of God's grandeur. Reflecting upon God, like Job, we feel the awe and reverence due a God who moves mountains, shakes the earth, and commands the sun. And yet we must pause to consider that this same powerful God holds each of us tenderly in the palm of his hand.

Job 9:1–12,14–16
Psalm 88:10bc–11,12–13,14–15
Matthew 18:1–5,10

Thursday

OCTOBER 3

Hear, O LORD, the sound of my call.
—PSALM 27:7A

We often struggle with prayer: How shall I pray? What methods or words should I use? When should I pray? How often should I pray? We can worry so much about praying that we end up *not* praying. What we need to know is that anytime we *try* to pray, we are praying. Even when we struggle, God hears our prayers. There is no wrong way to pray. However, God is not Santa Claus, so treating prayer as a Christmas wish list may not bring us the depth of prayer we seek. Even so, letting God know what we want and need is good. In the end, prayer doesn't change God; it changes us.

Job 19:21–27
Psalm 27:7–8a,8b–9abc,13–14
Luke 10:1–12

If I take the wings of the dawn,
if I settle at the farthest limits of the sea.
—PSALM 139:9

As a young man, I had a fierce devotion to St. Francis. I visited Assisi when I was twenty. From the moment I stepped off the train at the Basilica of St. Mary of the Angels, I felt the spirit of the Lord strongly. It was present when I walked those rolling hills surrounding Assisi. It was with me when I prayed in the cave hermitage where Francis prayed. And it was with me when I visited the hallowed grounds of San Damiano. Great saints like Francis may pass on, but they leave behind a spirit of love. I've kept that spirit with me ever since.

Job 38:1,12–21; 40:3–5
Psalm 139:1–3,7–8,9–10,13–14ab
Luke 10:13–16

I had heard of you by word of mouth,
but now my eye has seen you.
Therefore I disown what I have said,
and repent in dust and ashes.
—JOB 42:5–6

Biblical scholars have been debating the last words of Job for a long time. What they mean exactly, no one is sure. But a reasoned reading of the book of Job and a basic understanding of human nature points to this: Knowing God indirectly is not knowing God, and knowing God directly changes everything. From the moment we encounter God directly, we disown our past, repent, and surrender to the will of God: thy will be done, not mine.

Job 42:1–3,5–6,12–17
Psalm 119:66,71,75,91,125,130
Luke 10:17–24

Amen, I say to you,
whoever does not accept the kingdom of God like a child
will not enter it.
—MARK 10:15

By the time we're adults, we've played the game of life so
long that we may be too calculating to enter the kingdom of
God. We've forgotten that God's rules and the rules of the
world are very different. The world offers a zero-sum reality,
where everyone needs to fight for their piece. By contrast,
God offers endless generosity and unconditional love.
Perhaps that's why we need the simplicity and purity of being
children to believe this. It sounds too good to be true,
but it is.

Genesis 2:18–24
Psalm 128:1–2,3,4–5,6
Hebrews 2:9–11
Mark 10:2–16 or 10:2–12

Monday

OCTOBER 7

• OUR LADY OF THE ROSARY •

But because he wished to justify himself, he said to Jesus,
"And who is my neighbor?"
—LUKE 10:29

The two great commandments of Jesus are to love God with
all our heart and soul, and to love our neighbors as ourselves.
A scholar of the law attempts to trip up Jesus by asking him
to define "neighbor." Jesus tells the parable of the Good
Samaritan in response. A man, presumed to be Jewish, is
attacked and beaten by robbers and left by the side of the
road. Several Jews pass by the man without offering aid.
Only a Samaritan, despised by the Jews, stops to help. Jesus
is making a point to his Jewish audience—and us. Despite
our differences, we are all each other's neighbors.

Galatians 1:6–12
Psalm 111:1b–2,7–8,9 and 10c
Luke 10:25–37

⇒ 310 ⇐

Tuesday

OCTOBER 8

[Jesus said,] "There is need of only one thing."
—LUKE 10:42A

These are the words of Jesus, spoken to Martha, who is upset at her sister, Mary, for not helping her serve her guests, including Jesus. This is one of the most famous stories in the Gospels. The Martha/Mary paradox. Jesus seems to gently come down on the Mary side of things. But in truth, we are all a little bit Martha, and we are a little bit Mary, and we need to balance the two sides of our natures. Mary should help her sister prepare dinner and attend the guests so Martha can enjoy things as well. Martha needs to chill. We need to come together and be present to God among us, while still making sure we don't burn dinner.

Galatians 1:13–24
Psalm 139:1b–3,13–14ab,14c–15
Luke 10:38–42

• ST. DENIS, BISHOP, AND COMPANIONS, MARTYRS • ST. JOHN LEONARDI, PRIEST •

[Jesus taught them to pray,] "And forgive us our sins
for we ourselves forgive everyone in debt to us,
and do not subject us to the final test."
—LUKE 11:4

Here we read the "final test" ending to the Lord's Prayer
rather than the more common "but deliver us from evil."
What is the final test? It sounds ominous. Could the final test
be resisting the temptations of the world? Money, control,
lust, fame, power, or maybe thinking we can find happiness
and meaning without God? Whatever the "final test" may be,
I'm pretty sure none of us wants to take it. Look around:
everything in this world will end. Meanwhile, God offers us
eternal life and a place with him in heaven. Maybe the final
test challenges us to accept this incredible truth.

Galatians 2:1–2,7–14
Psalm 117:1bc,2
Luke 11:1–4

[Jesus said,] "I tell you, if he does not get up to give him the loaves
because of their friendship,
he will get up to give him whatever he needs
because of his persistence."
—LUKE 11:8

Jesus is encouraging his disciples to be persistent. Being
persistent is not often seen as a requirement for following
Jesus, but it's clear from this passage and others that Jesus
certainly thinks it's important. Persistence is defined as a
certain kind of doggedness or ability to see things through. A
persistent person is someone who has a vision or purpose in
mind that inspires and moves them. They are often dreamers
and visionaries who see their lives as governed by a higher
purpose. Persistent people like the apostle Paul, Francis of
Assisi, Ignatius of Loyola, and Mother Teresa.

Galatians 3:1–5
Luke 1:69–70,71–72,73–75
Luke 11:5–13

Brothers and sisters:
Realize that it is those who have faith
who are children of Abraham.
—GALATIANS 3:7

In Paul's time, as the Good News was being spread, various
communities would descend into scrupulous battles about
who could be an "approved" follower of Christ and who
could not. This was a constant challenge to Paul and the
early disciples. Paul addressed this by offering a simple litmus
test: anybody who believed in Christ Jesus, who loved the
Lord, and followed in his ways was an "approved" follower.
For Paul, the community of faith that began with God's
promise to Abraham was fulfilled through the cross, by the
death and resurrection of Christ Jesus. He didn't get caught
up in the minor details. Paul pointed to the cross and said,
"Through him, with him, and in him."

Galatians 3:7–14
Psalm 111:1b–2,3–4,5–6
Luke 11:15–26

While Jesus was speaking,
a woman from the crowd called out and said to him,
"Blessed is the womb that carried you
and the breasts at which you nursed."
He replied, "Rather, blessed are those
who hear the word of God and observe it."
—LUKE 11:27–28

The above passage from Luke is the complete Gospel reading for this day of the liturgical year. It's short, but notice how Jesus makes his point: even Mary, the mother of our Lord, with her proximity to Jesus, is no more blessed than anyone else who listens to the word of God and acts in accordance with the word. I'm not sure that's what the woman who called out to Jesus expected to hear, but it's certainly good news for all of us.

Galatians 3:22–29
Psalm 105:2–3,4–5,6–7
Luke 11:27–28

Teach us to number our days aright,
that we may gain wisdom of heart.
—PSALM 90:12

Recently, I celebrated my birthday. I'm older now than my
forty-year-old self could ever imagine, and you know what, I
feel great, and I'm doing well, thank the Lord. My wife asked
me if I felt any different yesterday than I did a year ago, and I
told her no, not at all. The only difference, if I'm being
honest, is the gratitude I feel for the life I've had. This
morning, during my prayers and devotional reading, I came
across the perfect sentiment for this year's birthday: Lord, it's
not important how much time I have left. All that's important
is what I do with the time I have left. Amen.

Wisdom 7:7–11
Psalm 90:12–13,14–15,16–17 (14)
Hebrews 4:12–13
Mark 10:17–30 or 10:17–27

Monday

OCTOBER 14

• ST. CALLISTUS I, POPE AND MARTYR •

Praise, you servants of the LORD,
praise the name of the LORD.
Blessed be the name of the LORD
both now and forever.
—PSALM 113:1B–2

Reason #13 for Going to Church

We go to church to praise God and to hear the Good News proclaimed. Recently, our retired diocesan bishop was filling in while our pastor was out on a medical emergency. The bishop is a compelling speaker, but what sets him apart is how he breaks open the Scriptures and applies them to our everyday lives. It was a blessing to hear this servant of the Lord speak from his heart. He was knowledgeable and inspiring. So, Reason #13 for Going to Church is the gift and grace of an unexpectedly great homily.

Galatians 4:22–24,26–27,31—5:1
Psalm 113:1b–2,3–4,5a and 6–7
Luke 11:29–32

OCTOBER 15

The Lord said to him, "Oh you Pharisees!
Although you cleanse the outside of the cup and the dish,
inside you are filled with plunder and evil.
You fools!
Did not the maker of the outside also make the inside?"
—LUKE 11:39–40

My father was in the cattle business in Texas during the 1970s. Cattlemen would sometimes refer derisively to someone as "big hat, no cattle." This meant someone who was all show and no substance. Jesus had a low threshold of tolerance for show-offs and hypocrites. But it is one thing for a businessman to inflate his net worth, and quite another for a religious leader to be a hypocrite in word and deed. Perhaps that's why Jesus calls them out some eighteen times in Scripture.

Galatians 5:1–6
Psalm 119:41,43,44,45,47,48
Luke 11:37–41

OCTOBER 16

If we live in the Spirit, let us also follow the Spirit.
—GALATIANS 5:25

What does Paul mean that "if we live in the Spirit, let us also follow in the Spirit"? The best analogy may be found in dance. When we dance with a partner, especially one who knows all the right moves, we allow ourselves to be led. It doesn't mean we're not fully participating; it just means we're taking our cues from our partner and letting them lead. It's a beautiful thing to watch a couple dance together who are in perfect sync. The spiritual path is something like this. We let the Spirit lead, but we're with the Spirit every step in the dance, and it's a beautiful thing.

Galatians 5:18–25
Psalm 1:1–2,3,4 and 6
Luke 11:42–46

Thursday

OCTOBER 17

• ST. IGNATIUS OF ANTIOCH, BISHOP AND MARTYR •

In all wisdom and insight, he has made known to us
the mystery of his will in accord with his favor
that he set forth in him as a plan for the fullness of times,
to sum up all things in Christ, in heaven and on earth.
—EPHESIANS 1:9–10

The good news of Christ is staggering. It can make our heads
spin trying to grasp what Paul is saying: Christ was God's
plan before the world began; the past, the present, and the
future all come together in Christ; the mystery of God's will
for creation is revealed in Christ; all things in heaven and
earth will be summed up in Christ; God has made this
known, through Christ, to those who believe. Got it?

Ephesians 1:1–10
Psalm 98:1,2–3ab,3cd–4,5–6
Luke 11:47–54

⇒ 320 ⇐

He said to them,
"The harvest is abundant but the laborers are few."
—LUKE 10:2

We are the laborers Jesus is speaking about, and the world
and all who live in it are the harvest. What does Jesus want
us to do? It's quite simple: proclaim the Good News to
everyone who is willing to hear it. For those who won't
listen, bless them and move on. Salvation is news worth
proclaiming. This is what made Albert Schweitzer become a
medical missionary in Africa. This is why Mother Teresa took
to the streets of Calcutta; and this is why Chris Tomlin's
songs are sung every week in churches around the world.
They all chose to become laborers to proclaim the
Good News.

2 Timothy 4:10–17b
Psalm 145:10–11,12–13,17–18
Luke 10:1–9

OCTOBER 19

• ST. JOHN DE BRÉBEUF AND ST. ISAAC JOGUES, PRIESTS,
AND COMPANIONS, MARTYRS •

Jesus said to his disciples:
"I tell you,
everyone who acknowledges me before others
the Son of Man will acknowledge before the angels of God."
—LUKE 12:8

Fr. Brébeuf and Fr. Jogues were French Jesuits who ministered
to the tribes of North America during the 1640s. What is
extraordinary about both Brébeuf and Jogues is how much
they suffered for the faith before making their way back to
France. They had been tortured and maimed and could have
stayed comfortably safe at home in Europe. But both chose
to return to North America and continue to proclaim the
Good News, though both were eventually martyred. We can
be assured the Son of Man acknowledged them before all the
angels of God.

Ephesians 1:15–23
Psalm 8:2–3ab,4–5,6–7
Luke 12:8–12

———————

James and John, the sons of Zebedee, came to Jesus and said to him,
"Teacher, we want you to do for us whatever we ask of you."
He replied, "What do you wish me to do for you?"
—MARK 10:35–36

Imagine the gall of James and John! Imagine speaking to Jesus
that way: "Hey, Lord, we need you to do whatever we need
you to do." The other apostles become disgusted with the
preening ambition of James and John. But Jesus doesn't
chastise the two; he reframes the discussion. Jesus teaches
them that power is found in service, and it means putting
others first and yourself last. To their credit, James and John
learn this lesson, and after years of fruitful service, they both
die heroically proclaiming this truth.

Isaiah 53:10–11
Psalm 33:4–5,18–19,20,22 (22)
Hebrews 4:14–16
Mark 10:35–45 or 10:42–45

Then he said to the crowd,
"Take care to guard against all greed,
for though one may be rich,
one's life does not consist of possessions."
—LUKE 12:15

I once got to know an extraordinary priest from India. He came to the United States later in life and was stunned by our materialism. He often challenged his audiences to consider whether they owned their possessions or their possessions owned them. For Lent one year, he asked the parish to bring any unwanted possessions they had to the church parking lot, where they could be given away to others who might need them. The result was so overwhelmingly popular, the church did it every Lent thereafter. Our possessions anchor us to this world when our focus should be on the next.

Ephesians 2:1–10
Psalm 100:1b–2,3,4ab,4c–5
Luke 12:13–21

OCTOBER 22

• ST. JOHN PAUL II, POPE •

I will hear what God proclaims;
the LORD—for he proclaims peace.
—PSALM 85:9A

I worked on a book by Pope John Paul II called *Go in Peace*.
The book was published around the time of the pope's death,
and an energetic publicist thought I should be on every news
outlet she could get me on. I was nervous at first and felt like
an imposter. I was a lowly book editor. I wasn't a theologian,
a papal biographer, or a church scholar. But the story of John
Paul II was so incredible that I felt privileged to share it.

Whenever I spoke, I felt the words flow through me. I
learned that when the Lord wants you to proclaim, he will
give you the words to do so.

Ephesians 2:12–22
Psalm 85:9ab–10,11–12,13–14
Luke 12:35–38

⋺ 325 ⋵

Wednesday

OCTOBER 23

God indeed is my savior;
I am confident and unafraid.
My strength and my courage is the LORD,
and he has been my savior.
—ISAIAH 12:2A

Are we truly confident and unafraid? Fear gets its power from our turning away, from our not facing what we are afraid of. Fear is a kind of blindness of our own choosing. We lack confidence when we lack conviction, when we make half-hearted choices, when we live tepidly, without passion or purpose. If God is indeed my savior, and Jesus suffered, was crucified, died, and rose from the dead, and I proclaim my belief in this miracle, how can I ever lack confidence or be afraid? What else does the Lord have to do to prove his saving love for me?

Ephesians 3:2–12
Isaiah 12:2–3,4bcd,5–6
Luke 12:39–48

Thursday

OCTOBER 24

• ST. ANTHONY MARY CLARET, BISHOP •

And that Christ may dwell in your hearts through faith;
that you, rooted and grounded in love,
may have strength to comprehend with all the holy ones
what is the breadth and length and height and depth,
and to know the love of Christ that surpasses knowledge,
so that you may be filled with all the fullness of God.
—EPHESIANS 3:17–19

When Christ dwells in our hearts and we are grounded and rooted in his love, we will know the peace that surpasses anything this world offers. And we will know that we are forgiven, rescued, redeemed, and saved. He will strengthen us to do more than we can ever imagine, and he will work through us to bring the power and glory of God to heaven and earth.

Ephesians 3:14–21
Psalm 33:1–2,4–5,11–12,18–19
Luke 12:49–53

You hypocrites!
You know how to interpret the appearance of the earth and the sky;
why do you not know how to interpret the present time?
—LUKE 12:56

Jesus sounds a little fierce here. What does he mean about interpreting the present time? It's possible he's speaking about *chronos* and *kairos*, two ancient Greek words referring to concepts of time. Chronos is sequential, normal clock time. Kairos means significant time, a charged time when something meaningful and momentous can happen, even something dangerous and cataclysmic. Jesus may be saying to the people that watching the weather is well and good, but paying attention to the deeper signs of the times might be more critical. Like recognizing the presence of the Messiah. Like recognizing the need for repentance. Like recognizing the kingdom of God is at hand.

Ephesians 4:1–6
Psalm 24:1–2,3–4ab,5–6
Luke 12:54–59

OCTOBER 26

Brothers and sisters:
Grace was given to each of us
according to the measure of Christ's gift.
—EPHESIANS 4:7

All the faithful receive the saving grace of Christ's sacrifice (gift), and for each of us, the grace is in accordance with our needs and talents. The church, the Body of Christ, has need of all our gifts and talents. We bring them to fullness in the service of the Body of Christ. In St. Paul's evolving theology of the early church, there were no special people or positions because everyone was necessary, everyone added something essential to the growing community of the faithful. While hierarchies are inevitable in the development of institutions, it is important to embrace the vision Paul had for the church at the beginning. All are welcome; all are important.

Ephesians 4:7–16
Psalm 122:1–2,3–4ab,4cd–5
Luke 13:1–9

Sunday

OCTOBER 27

• THIRTIETH SUNDAY IN ORDINARY TIME •

They departed in tears,
but I will console them and guide them;
I will lead them to brooks of water,
on a level road, so that none shall stumble.
—JEREMIAH 31:9A

God is always calling us home, calling us back to his
embrace. In this passage from Jeremiah, he is not only calling
us back home but also consoling us along the way. He's
guiding us and making sure we have fresh water and smooth
roads so we don't stumble and fall. God wants us back as
much as we want to be back.

Jeremiah 31:7–9
Psalm 126:1–2,2–3,4–5,6 (3)
Hebrews 5:1–6
Mark 10:46–52

Monday

OCTOBER 28

• ST. SIMON AND ST. JUDE, APOSTLES •

Jesus went up to the mountain to pray,
and he spent the night in prayer to God.
—LUKE 6:12

I've been outlining a book on prayer that I hope to write someday. As a result, I've collected quotes about prayer in Scripture, like the one above, and others from across the spectrum of Christian writers. Like Phillips Brooks, an Anglican clergyman in nineteenth-century Boston. He wrote some seriously great sermons, and his work remains relevant and inspiring to Christian devotional readers today. Among my favorite quotes from Reverend Brooks is this one: "Never pray for an easier life; pray to be a stronger person!"

Ephesians 2:19–22
Psalm 19:2–3,4–5
Luke 6:12–16

Jesus said, "What is the Kingdom of God like?
To what can I compare it?
It is like a mustard seed that a man took and planted in the garden.
When it was fully grown, it became a large bush
and the birds of the sky dwelt in its branches."
—LUKE 13:18–19

A river starts as a trickle of water. A trickle of water can, over time, create massive canyons and carve its way through high mountains. A human life starts with the fusing of two tiny, microscopic cells. The tallest tree in the forest begins from a small seed. From humble beginnings grow mighty things. The kingdom of God is like a small candle in your heart, and the flame of faith you nurture spreads outward into the world, until the whole world catches fire.

Ephesians 5:21–33
Psalm 128:1–2,3,4–5
Luke 13:18–21

Someone asked him,
"Lord, will only a few people be saved?"
He answered them,
"Strive to enter through the narrow gate,
for many, I tell you, will attempt to enter
but will not be strong enough."
—LUKE 13:23

First, the good news regarding salvation: there is a door, and many will try to enter even though the door is narrow. Some may not be strong enough, but Jesus encourages all to "strive to enter." The bad news is that many of us are not paying attention, we're not making good choices, and we lack the focus and sense of urgency necessary to understand the reality of our situation. In A.A. (Alcoholics Anonymous) they say, "You have to participate in your own recovery." I hear Jesus saying, "I'm here to help, but you have to participate in your own salvation."

Ephesians 6:1–9
Psalm 145:10–11,12–13ab,13cd–14
Luke 13:22–30

Thursday

OCTOBER 31

*With all prayer and supplication,
pray at every opportunity in the Spirit.*
—EPHESIANS 6:18

Pope Benedict XVI wrote, "Paul teaches us another important thing: he says that there is no true prayer without the presence of the Spirit within us. . . . In Paul's opinion . . . the Spirit stirs us to the very depths of our being." Praying in the Spirit for St. Paul was praying on steroids. The language of the Spirit was a direct conduit to God and created a supercharged form of communication between the divine and the human.

Ephesians 6:10–20
Psalm 144:1b,2,9–10
Luke 13:31–35

NOVEMBER 1

• ALL SAINTS •

Beloved, we are God's children now;
what we shall be has not yet been revealed.
We do know that when it is revealed we shall be like him,
for we shall see him as he is.
—1 JOHN 3:2

Today, the church honors all the known saints who are in
heaven. My mother raised me to have a deep respect for the
saints of our church. In fact, she had shelves of books on the
saints, their stories, and their writings. Her favorite saint was
Mary, Mother of God. I asked my mother once why she was
so interested in the saints. She looked at me and said, "Well,
because I want to be a saint, of course."

Revelation 7:2–4,9–14
Psalm 24:1bc–2,3–4ab,5–6
1 John 3:1–3
Matthew 5:1–12a

NOVEMBER 2

• THE COMMEMORATION OF ALL THE FAITHFUL DEPARTED
(ALL SOULS' DAY) •

The souls of the just are in the hand of God.
—WISDOM 3:1A

Reason #27 for going to church

Around All Souls' Day, many parishes have a Mass of
Remembrance. This special liturgy honors those in the parish
who have died in the previous year. Family and friends bring
a framed photograph of the departed, which is set on a
special table at the front of the church. After the homily,
family members come forward, light a votive candle from the
paschal candle, and place them beside their loved ones'
pictures while offering a prayer. There is open grieving, tears,
and hugs, but when Mass is over, you catch a few shy smiles
and sense that hearts have been lightened and lifted.

Wisdom 3:1–9
Romans 5:5–11 or 6:3–9
John 6:37–40
Other readings may be selected.

[Moses said,] "Therefore, you shall love the LORD, your God,
with all your heart,
and with all your soul,
and with all your strength."
—DEUTERONOMY 6:5–6

These are powerful words from Moses to the Israelites.
Moses was a visionary, and he created a new world. A world
with one God and a covenant between that one God,
Yahweh, and his chosen people, the Jews. Moses is a sacred
figure in multiple religious traditions, his story epic. The first
five books of the Bible are attributed to him. He led his
people from captivity and slavery to freedom in the Promised
Land. As Christians, we find the fulfillment of our salvation
story in Jesus. But not without Moses and the Exodus. The
journey from slavery to the Promised Land is our story too.

Deuteronomy 6:2–6
Psalm 18:2–3,3–4,47,51 (2)
Hebrews 7:23–28
Mark 12:28b–34

Monday

NOVEMBER 4

• ST. CHARLES BORROMEO, BISHOP •

Brothers and sisters:
If there is any encouragement in Christ,
any solace in love,
any participation in the Spirit,
any compassion and mercy,
complete my joy by being of the same mind, with the same love,
united in heart, thinking one thing.
—PHILIPPIANS 2:1–2

Paul was in prison while writing this, which makes the gentle, compassionate tone here even more remarkable. He invokes at least four of his go-to themes here: the encouragement we find in Christ's love; the actions of the Spirit on our behalf; the joy in Christian unity; and the "thinking one thing," which for Paul means leaving behind the past, not worrying about the future, and focusing on the will of God in this moment. Advice specific to the first-century church that sounds like good advice for the twenty-first-century church.

Philippians 2:1–4
Psalm 131:1bcde,2,3
Luke 14:12–14

NOVEMBER 5

"For, I tell you, none of those men who were invited will taste my dinner."
—LUKE 14:24

One of the most influential writers I worked with was Fr. William Barry. Bill wrote a number of foundational Ignatian spirituality works, but he told me that almost all his books had one simple idea: God wants to be our friend. The words above are spoken by the master in the parable of the great feast. A wealthy man invites his friends to a special dinner, and all of them find excuses not to attend. Imagine how you might feel if you threw a dinner for your friends and nobody came! Now imagine that God threw a dinner party for us but none of us went. It's no way to treat a friend, and it's certainly no way to treat God.

Philippians 2:5–11
Psalm 22:26b–27,28–30ab,30e,31–32
Luke 14:15–24

NOVEMBER 6

For God is the one who, for his good purpose,
works in you both to desire and to work.
—PHILIPPIANS 2:13

Working out our salvation is what we are here to do. We don't do this on our own. Salvation requires that we align our will to God's desires for us. We do this through prayer, worship, acts of mercy and generosity, kindness, and love. We do this through the good work of kingdom building. Each of us is called to do our part, but we have to want to do it—the desire—and we have to make the effort—the work. God will do the rest.

Philippians 2:12–18
Psalm 27:1,4,13–14
Luke 14:25–33

NOVEMBER 7

[Jesus said,] "I tell you, in just the same way
there will be more joy in heaven over one sinner who repents
than over ninety-nine righteous people
who have no need of repentance."
—LUKE 15:7

What kind of God cares more about the one who is lost than the ninety-nine who are all safe and accounted for? Our God. What kind of God celebrates one sinner finding their way to repentance while ninety-nine righteous souls have already found their way home? Our God. What kind of math is at work here? God's math. In the arithmetic of God, the only measure is love.

Philippians 3:3–8a
Psalm 105:2–3,4–5,6–7
Luke 15:1–10

Their minds are occupied with earthly things.
But our citizenship is in heaven.
—PHILIPPIANS 3:19B–20A

We are like travelers visiting a foreign country that we've
learned to call home. We know this place, and we've made a
life here. But we also know that someday we will return to
the place of our origin, the place that is our true home. Paul
didn't want the early faithful to become so distracted with
where they were that they forgot where they were going.
This life of faith is a journey for followers of Jesus, a journey
that leads us home to heaven. Fixing our eyes on the Lord,
having a clarity of purpose, praying for the necessary graces,
all help us keep our minds occupied and oriented towards the
heavenly while living in the earthly.

Philippians 3:17—4:1
Psalm 122:1–2,3–4ab,4cd–5
Luke 16:1–8

God is our refuge and our strength,
an ever-present help in distress.
—PSALM 46:2

The most powerful and seductive lie I can succumb to is the lie that I am the center of the universe. The most powerful and persuasive antidote to that lie is my acknowledging that God is the center of the universe. All the struggles of my life occur when I forget the truth and believe the lie.

Ezekiel 47:1–2,8–9,12
Psalm 46:2–3,5–6,8–9
1 Corinthians 3:9c–11,16–17
John 2:13–22

[Jesus] sat down opposite the treasury
and observed how the crowd put money into the treasury.
Many rich people put in large sums.
A poor widow also came and put in two small coins worth a few cents.
Calling his disciples to himself, he said to them,
"Amen, I say to you, this poor widow put in more
than all the other contributors to the treasury.
For they have all contributed from their surplus wealth,
but she, from her poverty, has contributed all she had,
her whole livelihood."
—MARK 12:41–44

It's easy to give of what we have in abundance, but it's quite
another thing to give the last of what we have. One requires
no faith; the other requires total faith.

1 Kings 17:10–16
Psalm 146:7,8–9,9–10 (1b)
Hebrews 9:24–28
Mark 12:38–44 or 12:41–44

NOVEMBER 11

• ST. MARTIN OF TOURS, BISHOP •

The Lord replied, "If you have faith the size of a mustard seed,
you would say to this mulberry tree,
'Be uprooted and planted in the sea,' and it would obey you."
—LUKE 17:6

We may be tempted to focus on the more sensational second part of what Jesus says here, but I believe the real message lies in realizing how a little faith can go a long way. Jesus is saying that what begins very small can grow into something quite large. The point is how faith expands us, allows us to take root and grow. If God chooses to uproot a mulberry tree and plant it in the sea, then God can do it. But only faith allows us to believe that. Faith makes the unbelievable possible.

Titus 1:1–9
Psalm 24:1b–2,3–4ab,5–6
Luke 17:1–6

Tuesday

NOVEMBER 12

• ST. JOSAPHAT, BISHOP AND MARTYR •

Beloved:
You must say what is consistent with sound doctrine,
namely, that older men should be temperate, dignified,
self-controlled, sound in faith, love, and endurance.
—TITUS 2:1–2

The older we get, the more we need to realize there is only so much time left for us to be the better people God is calling us to be. Age does not automatically confer wisdom, but experience should. The task of older men is to be a blessing to the people in their lives, especially the younger people. When a man reaches a certain age, time and circumstance should have tempered him. He should choose a path of generativity. The wiser men among us know that our later years are best spent as rainmakers, making possible the dreams of others.

Titus 2:1–8,11–14
Psalm 37:3–4,18 and 23,27 and 29
Luke 17:7–10

NOVEMBER 13

• ST. FRANCES XAVIER CABRINI, VIRGIN •

Even though I walk in the dark valley,
I fear no evil; for you are at my side.
—PSALM 23:4

In Psalm 23, the psalmist says, "I fear no evil." In the Lord's
Prayer, Jesus ends with "deliver us from evil." Evil is real, and
we are foolish to deny it. It was real for the Old Testament
psalmist, and it was real for our Lord in the New Testament.
As we watch the evening news, it is obvious that evil is still
around us today. But for those who believe, with God at our
side, we need not fear the evil in the world. God is our
protection and our deliverance. But implicit in this is that we
stay close to God and far from evil.

Titus 3:1–7
Psalm 23:1b–3a,3bc–4,5,6
Luke 17:11–19

Jesus said in reply,
"The coming of the Kingdom of God cannot be observed,
and no one will announce, 'Look, here it is,' or, 'There it is.'
For behold, the Kingdom of God is among you."
—LUKE 17:20–21

Jesus says we cannot see the kingdom of God, yet it is here and it is among us. But what is the kingdom of God we cannot see? Maybe we glimpse the kingdom in the kindness of the volunteer at the food pantry or in the gentle care of a hospice worker or in the smile of a stranger. Maybe the kingdom *is* kindness, compassion, and love, breaking through the fear and the darkness. Maybe the kingdom of God *is* all around us, and we simply need to notice.

Philemon 7–20
Psalm 146:7,8–9a,9bc–10
Luke 17:20–25

For this is love, that we walk according to his commandments;
this is the commandment, as you heard from the beginning,
in which you should walk.
—2 JOHN 6

Love is an emotion. Love is a decision. Love is an action.
Love is a direction. Love is a choice to live in a certain way.
This is what John says in the passage above. When we keep
the commandments of the Lord, to love God and to love our
neighbor, we are committing to a course of action, a way of
being in the world: a way of love.

2 John 4–9
Psalm 119:1,2,10,11,17,18
Luke 17:26–37

Saturday

NOVEMBER 16

• ST. MARGARET OF SCOTLAND * ST. GERTRUDE THE GREAT, VIRGIN •

Beloved, you are faithful in all you do for the brothers and sisters,
especially for strangers;
they have testified to your love before the Church.
Please help them in a way worthy of God to continue their journey.
—3 JOHN 5–6

This Third Letter of John is one of the briefest selections in
the Bible. It is concerned with the conduct of two
first-century church leaders and their communities. One
leader was a decent, good man; the other was creating some
difficulties. What makes it relevant to us today and worthy of
our attention is John's effort to find a healing solution to the
faith communities in crisis. John knew our faith journey is a
shared one, and we are called to walk together—then,
and now.

3 John 5–8
Psalm 112:1–2,3–4,5–6
Luke 18:1–8

Sunday

NOVEMBER 17

• THIRTY-THIRD SUNDAY IN ORDINARY TIME •

[Jesus said,] "Heaven and earth will pass away,
but my words will not pass away."
—MARK 13:31

Jesus lived some two thousand years ago. The entire population of the world was three hundred million. He was born in a small village in a remote corner of the Roman Empire. He was poor, home-schooled. His public ministry was brief. He never wrote a book. He survived on temp work and charity. He didn't found a formal movement. His entire message can be summed up by "Love God fiercely, and love your neighbor as yourself." But his influence can be seen in art, architecture, law, education, politics, and the lives of many of the greatest souls throughout history. Also, in the over two billion people who consider themselves his followers today—no, his words have not passed away.

Daniel 12:1–3
Psalm 16:5,8,9–10,11 (1)
Hebrews 10:11–14,18
Mark 13:24–32

NOVEMBER 18

• THE DEDICATION OF THE BASILICA OF ST. PETER AND ST. PAUL, APOSTLES
• ST. ROSE PHILIPPINE DUCHESNE, VIRGIN •

Then Jesus stopped and ordered that he be brought to him;
and when he came near, Jesus asked him.
"What do you want me to do for you?"
He replied, "Lord, please let me see."
Jesus told him, "Have sight; your faith has saved you."
—LUKE 18:40–42

"What do you want me to do for you?" When you pray and ask Jesus for something, Jesus will ask you in return the same thing he asked the blind beggar: "What do you want me to do for you?" What will your answer be?

Revelation 1:1–4; 2:1–5 or Acts 28:11–16,30–31
Psalm 1:1–2,3,4 and 6 or 98:1,2–3ab,3cd–4,5–6
Luke 18:35–43 or Matthew 14:22–33

NOVEMBER 19

[Jesus said,] "Behold, I stand at the door and knock."
—REVELATION 3:20

Hospitality is important for the people of the Bible. It is not only a custom of desert society; it is a spiritual and cultural practice. The welcoming of the stranger, alms for the needy, food and drink for the hungry and thirsty—these actions recognize our common needs, our interdependence, and our shared humanity. Throughout Scripture, from Abraham to Jesus, hospitality is intrinsic to the behavior of God's chosen people. In Hebrews 13, the author suggests that when we show hospitality to strangers, we may be entertaining angels. Consider the stranger at your door, the one you invite in, the one you share a meal with. Perhaps you will recognize that stranger in the future, as an angel, or Jesus himself, when sharing a meal at heaven's banquet.

Revelation 3:1–6,14–22
Psalm 15:2–3a,3bc–4ab,5
Luke 19:1–10

Wednesday

NOVEMBER 20

*Let everything that has breath
praise the LORD! Alleluia.*
—PSALM 150:6

The psalmist's prayer is echoed in the First Principle and
Foundation from the Spiritual Exercises of St. Ignatius: "God
created human beings to praise, reverence, and serve God,
and by doing this, to save their souls." It goes on to say, "God
created all other things on the face of the earth to help fulfill
this purpose." It concludes with "and so in all the rest, so that
we ultimately desire and choose only what is most conducive
for us to the end for which God created us." Yes, "Let
everything that has breath praise the LORD! Alleluia!"

Revelation 4:1–11
Psalm 150:1b–2,3–4,5–6
Luke 19:11–28

NOVEMBER 21

• THE PRESENTATION OF THE BLESSED VIRGIN MARY •

As Jesus drew near Jerusalem,
he saw the city and wept over it, saying,
"If this day you only knew what makes for peace—
but now it is hidden from your eyes."
—LUKE 19:41–42

The above passage, referred to as the lament of Jerusalem, comes before the cleansing of the temple. Things were heating up around Jesus and his followers. He could feel his enemies drawing closer. After three years of teaching, performing miracles, and healing—and trying to help people see the truth—the end was near. Of course, Jesus would have grown saddened, disappointed, and emotionally drained. He was God, but he was human, and that human frailty would have been his greatest challenge during his final days.

Revelation 5:1–10
Psalm 149:1b–2,3–4,5–6a and 9b
Luke 19:41–44

The chief priests, the scribes, and the leaders of the people, meanwhile,
were seeking to put him to death,
but they could find no way to accomplish their purpose
because all the people were hanging on his words.
—LUKE 19:47–48

June 1979 was a dangerous time for Pope John Paul II. When
he returned to his beloved Poland, the Communist rulers
were nervous, the military on alert. In Krakow, John Paul II
said Mass to between two and three million people.
Hundreds of thousands gathered near his hotel later,
chanting his name. He could have told the people to rebel
against their unpopular leaders, and they would have done
it—"because all the people were hanging on his words."
Instead, he came out on his balcony, blessed the people, and
told them to return home and go to bed.

Revelation 10:8–11
Psalm 119:14,24,72,103,111,131
Luke 19:45–48

• ST. CLEMENT I, POPE AND MARTYR * ST. COLUMBAN, ABBOT * BLESSED
MIGUEL AUGUSTÍN PRO, PRIEST AND MARTYR •

*[Jesus said,] "And he is not God of the dead, but of the living,
for to him all are alive."*
—LUKE 20:38

One of the constant themes in the New Testament is the
fraught relationship between Jesus and the Sadducees and
how often they try to trip him up on Mosaic law, and how
invariably they cannot. In Luke 20, they try to catch him in
the proper application of laws regarding death, marriage,
wives, widows, and resurrection. Jesus sidesteps their
questions by telling them that in the next life, all distinctions
disappear and we become like angels, true spiritual children
of the Light. Grumbling, they walk away conceding his
point, and no doubt plotting their next argument.

Revelation 11:4–12
Psalm 144:1,2,9–10
Luke 20:27–40

NOVEMBER 24

• OUR LORD JESUS CHRIST, KING OF THE UNIVERSE •

"I am the Alpha and the Omega," says the Lord God,
"the one who is and who was and who is to come, the almighty."
—REVELATION 1:8

This last Sunday in Ordinary Time, we celebrate the
Solemnity of Christ, the King of the Universe. Today's
readings all reflect this theme. Begun nearly a century ago by
Pope Pius XI and refined by Pope Paul VI, the Solemnity was
in part an effort to meet the rising secularism of the
twentieth century. It was also a way for the church to speak
to the magnitude of Christ's reign as King. Simply put, Christ
is, was, and will be the forever revelation of God's universal
love. On this day we are called to reflect upon this
profound truth.

Daniel 7:13–14
Psalm 93:1,1–2,5 (1a)
Revelation 1:5–8
John 18:33b–37

NOVEMBER 25

• ST. CATHERINE OF ALEXANDRIA, VIRGIN AND MARTYR •

I heard a sound from heaven
like the sound of rushing water.
—REVELATION 14:2A

Yesterday was cold, the sky clear, and the late autumn sun blinding. My wife, Mary, and I decided to hike in the woods. We both like to pray when we hike. The air was still as we went silently up a steep rise and into a stand of conifers. We stopped in the shade of a large tree, in what appeared to be a dip in the trail. Out of the south, a rushing wind, like the sound of white water in the mountains, came up suddenly and blew right through us, and then subsided just as suddenly. Startled, I was just gathering my thoughts when I caught my wife whispering, "I hear you, Lord."

Revelation 14:1–3,4b–5
Psalm 24:1bc–2,3–4ab,5–6
Luke 21:1–4

NOVEMBER 26

Then shall all the trees of the forest exult.
—PSALM 96:12

I'm blessed to live near a forest preserve with a beautiful, clear lake. I walk there frequently, especially around sunset. While walking there and taking pictures, I've discovered that the light is remarkable. For years I've been taking pictures of the same majestic maple tree, which reflects beautifully on the water. I call it my tree of life. After hundreds of pictures of this same tree, I feel like I've come to know it. Observing it at different times of the day and year, I've noticed subtle changes. I do think trees reveal themselves, if you're patient enough—and I can assure you, trees do exult.

Revelation 14:14–19
Psalm 96:10,11–12,13
Luke 21:5–11

[Jesus said,] "By your perseverance you will secure your lives."
—LUKE 21:19

We don't often speak of the cost of discipleship. But Jesus acknowledged that the first disciples would face danger for proclaiming the Good News. He said they might be arrested, beaten, tortured, and even put to death. The cost of discipleship in the early church could be steep. And yet, by the end of the first century, some seventy-five hundred people were estimated to be followers of Jesus, and by the end of the second century, the number was over 200,000. Today it's over two billion. When Jesus said, "By your perseverance you will secure your lives," the early disciples believed it to be true and proclaimed the gospel with fearless devotion. Let us continue what they so bravely began.

Revelation 15:1–4
Psalm 98:1,2–3ab,7–8,9
Luke 21:12–19

NOVEMBER 28

Enter his gates with thanksgiving,
his courts with praise;
Give thanks to him; bless his name.
—PSALM 100:4

My favorite holiday of the year is Thanksgiving. It's the one day of the year we formally celebrate being grateful. If it were up to me, we would have Thanksgiving on the calendar once a month. Other than loving God and your neighbor as yourself, there is nothing more important than practicing gratitude. Meanwhile, thank you, Lord, for your many blessings, and help us to be mindful that every day should be a day of thanksgiving.

Revelation 18:1–2,21–23; 19:1–3,9a
Psalm 100:1b–2,3,4,5
Luke 21:20–28

PROPER MASS IN THANKSGIVING
TO GOD:
Sirach 50:22–24
1 Corinthians 1:3–9
Luke 17:11–19
for Thanksgiving Day, any readings from
the Mass "In Thanksgiving to God"
(943–947)

Then I saw a new heaven and a new earth.
—REVELATION 21:1A

The book of Revelation is mystical visionary writing, and it contains extraordinary passages. "And he said to me, It is done! I am the Alpha and the Omega, the beginning and the end" (Revelation 21:6). Also, "He will wipe away every tear from their eyes, and death shall be no more, neither shall there be mourning, nor crying, nor pain anymore, for the former things have passed away" (Revelation 21:4).

Essentially, Revelation describes the indescribable: the second coming of our Lord. When St. John writes that the Second Coming will be like "a new heaven and a new earth," he's saying, "Trust me, it will be so amazing, so incredible, it's like nothing you've ever seen before."

Revelation 20:1–4,11—21:2
Psalm 84:3,4,5–6a and 8a
Luke 21:29–33

NOVEMBER 30

· ST. ANDREW, APOSTLE ·

As Jesus was walking by the Sea of Galilee, he saw two brothers,
Simon who is called Peter, and his brother Andrew,
casting a net into the sea; they were fishermen.
He said to them,
"Come after me, and I will make you fishers of men."
At once they left their nets and followed him.
—MATTHEW 4:18–20

Reading this passage, I often put myself in the scene and wonder if I would drop my nets and follow this mysterious stranger, let alone have my brother also do it with me. I think one of us would have tried to talk the other one out of it by speaking to our responsibilities and commitments. I just can't see it happening, but then again, if I was looking into the eyes of Jesus and he said, "Come..." Well, maybe I would have thrown caution to the wind and done what Peter and Andrew did. The thing is, Jesus is always calling us to put down our nets and follow him.

Romans 10:9–18
Psalm 19:8,9,10,11
Matthew 4:18–22

The days are coming, says the LORD,
when I will fulfill the promise
I made to the house of Israel and Judah.
—JEREMIAH 33:14

Musician Tom Petty said that waiting is the hardest part. But as we begin with this first Sunday of Advent, like it or not, we are beginning our time of waiting—for the coming of Emmanuel, God with us. But unlike waiting in line at the DMV, this waiting is charged with hope and God's promise made to Israel and fulfilled to all of us with the birth of Jesus. God is bringing light into the darkness with the birth of the Christ child, a miracle worth the waiting.

Jeremiah 33:14–16
Psalm 25:4–5,8–9,10,14 (1b)
1 Thessalonians 3:12—4:2
Luke 21:25–28,34–36

DECEMBER 2

*The mountain of the LORD's house
shall be established as the highest mountain
and raised above the hills.*
—ISAIAH 2:2

In the past week, I've learned that a colleague of my son has been diagnosed with late-stage cancer. His medical insurance may run out because he can't work due to the severe complications of the treatment he requires. The sudden death of a young mother at church has left three bewildered young children and a grief-stricken husband behind. A good friend's neighbor, a struggling twelve-year-old boy, recently committed suicide. Life is full of storms and challenges, but history keeps moving toward glory and peace in God's presence. In the meantime, God is with us.

Isaiah 2:1–5
Psalm 122:1–2,3–4b,4cd–5,6–7,8–9
Matthew 8:5–11

Tuesday

DECEMBER 3

• ST. FRANCIS XAVIER, PRIEST •

The Spirit of the LORD shall rest upon him:
a Spirit of wisdom and of understanding,
A Spirit of counsel and of strength,
a Spirit of knowledge and of fear of the LORD.
—ISAIAH 11:2

Isaiah made this prophecy seven hundred years before the birth of Jesus. As we move through Advent and the Christmas season, we become aware of how many Old Testament readings point toward the coming King who would usher in a new world. The faithful spent centuries waiting, praying, and longing for the arrival of this new King. We might consider this as we move through several weeks rather than several centuries of waiting ourselves. Not to mention, we know the King has come and, in joyful hope, we know he will come again.

Isaiah 11:1–10
Psalm 72:1–2,7–8,12–13,17
Luke 10:21–24

⇒ 367 ⇐

On this mountain he will destroy
the veil that veils all peoples,
The web that is woven over all nations;
he will destroy death forever.
The Lord GOD will wipe away
the tears from all faces;
The reproach of his people he will remove
from the whole earth; for the LORD has spoken.

On that day it will be said:
"Behold our God, to whom we looked to save us!"
—ISAIAH 25:7–9

Isaiah tells us that the Lord God will destroy the veil that covers all nations, and he will destroy death and wipe away our tears. By the birth of an innocent child and the courage of a crucified man, this and more was accomplished.

Isaiah 25:6–10a
Psalm 23:1–3a,3b–4,5,6
Matthew 15:29–37

DECEMBER 5

Give thanks to the LORD, for he is good,
for his mercy endures forever.
—PSALM 118:1

I've always loved the question posed by the traditional
Christmas hymn "What Child Is This?" During this Advent
season, as we celebrate that first Christmas, let's consider just
some of the miraculous events surrounding our Lord's birth,
such as the Holy Family escaping Herod's murderous
intentions. The gift and grace of our Lord being born as an
innocent child. The love of two young people, new parents
who did not completely understand their roles but fully
embraced them. The recognition by simple shepherds of
something profound occurring in the most unlikely setting.
The affirmation of something momentous marked by the
arrival from afar, and the gifts of wise men and the star that
guided them. What child is this, indeed!

Isaiah 26:1–6
Psalm 118:1 and 8–9,19–21,25–27a
Matthew 7:21,24–27

Wait for the LORD with courage;
be stouthearted, and wait for the LORD.
—PSALM 27:14

Advent is a time of waiting, but it need not be a passive
waiting. Pray during Advent and in anticipation of the
coming of our Lord, using prayer to wait with purpose and
hope. Just as our Lord is bringing light into the darkness,
what can you do to help brighten someone else's life? Be the
light in the darkness by bringing the light into the life of
someone who needs it. Remain positive, knowing that the
One who changed everything is coming again and offers us
blessed assurance. Act with this assurance, blessing others
with your faith and trust. The good news of Advent needs to
be proclaimed and shared, actively not passively.

Isaiah 29:17–24
Psalm 27:1,4,13–14
Matthew 9:27–31

DECEMBER 7

• ST. AMBROSE, BISHOP AND DOCTOR OF THE CHURCH •

He will be gracious to you when you cry out,
as soon as he hears he will answer you.
—ISAIAH 30:19B

When my life was essentially crumbling around me, the emotional pain was almost more than I could bear. Each day was a struggle, a small victory to simply make it through. Each night I fell to my knees and thanked the Lord for getting me through the day and asked him to help me get through the next one. I can honestly say that, in the depths of my despair, I never felt closer to God. I have no desire to revisit the turmoil of that time, but I know that if I cry out to the Lord, he will answer.

Isaiah 30:19–21,23–26
Psalm 147:1–2,3–4,5–6
Matthew 9:35—10:1,5a,6–8

DECEMBER 8

• SECOND SUNDAY OF ADVENT •

And this is my prayer:
that your love may increase ever more and more
in knowledge and every kind of perception,
to discern what is of value,
so that you may be pure and blameless for the day of Christ.
—PHILIPPIANS 1:9–10

Paul prays that the community in Philippi increase in their love of God and one another. That they gain more knowledge of God working among them. That they perceive the movements of the Spirit and discern what is meaningful and important. That they should do these things as acts of purification and penance in preparation for the glorious second coming of our Lord. Of course, everything that Paul prays for in Philippi is his prayer for us today.

Baruch 5:1–9
Psalm 126:1–2,2–3,4–5,6 (3)
Philippians 1:4–6,8–11
Luke 3:1–6

DECEMBER 9

• THE IMMACULATE CONCEPTION OF THE BLESSED VIRGIN MARY (PATRONAL
FEAST DAY OF THE UNITED STATES OF AMERICA) •

And coming to her, he said,
"Hail, full of grace! The Lord is with you."
But she was greatly troubled at what was said
and pondered what sort of greeting this might be.
—LUKE 1:28–29

I found more than 120 words that mean the same thing as
"troubled," the word Luke uses to express how Mary was
feeling when the angel Gabriel told her the news. Among
them, *perplexed, worried, upset, anxious, nervous, uneasy, concerned,*
apprehensive, and *disturbed.* This word exercise helps us
consider and imagine the emotions of a brave young woman
facing this bewildering news and frightening angel. But the
only word that really counts is her *yes.* The one word that
made our salvation possible.

Genesis 3:9–15,20
Psalm 98:1,2–3ab,3cd–4
Ephesians 1:3–6,11–12
Luke 1:26–38

*In just the same way, it is not the will of your heavenly Father
that one of these little ones be lost.*
—MATTHEW 18:14

Jesus places a small child in the midst of the disciples and tells them that the child is one of the "little ones" and then refers to the child as the "greatest in the kingdom." Jesus goes on to issue a stark warning to anyone who might hurt these innocent "little ones." He follows this by telling the disciples the parable of the lost sheep and how all of heaven rejoices with the return of one lost person. His message is clear: all are beloved by God, even those we might deem the most insignificant—and our task is to look out for the lost, the little, and the innocent.

Isaiah 40:1–11
Psalm 96:1–2,3 and 10ac,11–12,13
Matthew 18:12–14

They that hope in the LORD will renew their strength,
they will soar as with eagles' wings.
—ISAIAH 40:31

"On Eagle's Wings" is a devotional hymn written in the late 1970s by Michael Joncas, a young Catholic priest. He wrote it for a friend whose father had died suddenly of a heart attack. It took some time for the song to gain popularity, but now it's among the most popular hymns in the world, especially at funerals. Anecdotally, people say they love the song but have a hard time singing it because it makes them cry. Perhaps people cry because they hope that, at the end of their life, the Lord will lift them up and help them soar toward heaven's gates on eagles' wings. I know I do.

Isaiah 40:25–31
Psalm 103:1–2,3–4,8 and 10
Matthew 11:28–30

Thursday

DECEMBER 12

• OUR LADY OF GUADALUPE •

Silence, all mankind, in the presence of the LORD!
For he stirs forth from his holy dwelling.
—ZECHARIAH 2:17

I find a certain holiness in walking in nature, especially
during winter. One morning last December, I woke early to
find the sun shining off several inches of newly fallen snow. I
put on my boots and warm clothes and headed to the forest.
The woods were quiet, a deep silence, and the snow as yet
undisturbed. I felt a sense of peaceful expectation in the
crisp, cold air. The snow had blanketed everything in a
mantle of grace. Advent is like that, the sense of holiness
descending and hopeful expectation. The Lord stirring from
his holy dwelling, soon to gift us with his beloved.

Zechariah 2:14–17 or Revelation 11:19a; 12:1–6a,10ab
Judith 13:18bcde,19
Luke 1:26–38 or 1:39–47

I, the LORD, your God,
teach you what is for your good,
and lead you on the way you should go.
—ISAIAH 48:17B

Thomas Merton, in his book *Thoughts in Solitude*, writes: "My Lord God, I have no idea where I am going. I do not see the road ahead of me. I cannot know for certain where it will end." But Merton commits to following the Lord nonetheless. He adds, "And I know that if I do this you will lead me by the right road, though I may know nothing about it." As Merton writes, we may not know the way we should go, but God does. The question for each of us is, "Will I let God lead me and show me where I should go?"

Isaiah 48:17–19
Psalm 1:1–2,3,4 and 6
Matthew 11:16–19

May your help be with the man of your right hand,
with the son of man whom you yourself made strong.
—PSALM 80:18

Today, the church honors St. John of the Cross, a Spanish
Carmelite priest and mystic who lived from 1542 to 1591.
He was a friend of St. Teresa of Ávila and a major figure in
the Catholic Counter-Reformation movement. He was a poet
and wrote two of the greatest spiritual classics of his age, *The
Dark Night of the Soul* and *Ascent of Mount Carmel*. His life was
an inspiration to many, and his wisdom is an enduring legacy:
"In the twilight of life, God will not judge us on our earthly
possessions and human success, but rather on how much we
have loved."

Sirach 48:1–4,9–11
Psalm 80:2ac and 3b,15–16,18–19
Matthew 17:9a,10–13

DECEMBER 15

• THIRD SUNDAY OF ADVENT •

Rejoice in the Lord always.
I shall say it again: rejoice!
Your kindness should be known to all.
The Lord is near.
Have no anxiety at all, but in everything,
by prayer and petition, with thanksgiving,
make your requests known to God.
Then the peace of God that surpasses all understanding
will guard your hearts and minds in Christ Jesus.
—PHILIPPIANS 4:4–7

In Philippians 4:4–7, St. Paul concisely lays out exactly how we should pray. Rejoice; God is near; try not to worry; be grateful; trust the peace you do not understand; and know that God is watching over you. I keep this passage with me always and read it often. I encourage you to keep Paul's words nearby and read them whenever the world becomes too much.

Zephaniah 3:14–18a
Isaiah 12:2–3,4,5–6 (6)
Philippians 4:4–7
Luke 3:10–18

DECEMBER 16

I see him, though not now;
I behold him, though not near:
—NUMBERS 24:17A

Teilhard de Chardin wrote, "Above all, trust in the slow work of God. We are quite naturally impatient in everything to reach the end without delay. We should like to skip the intermediate stages. We are impatient of being on the way to something unknown, something new." For some, Advent is an impatient waiting for the magic of Christmas morning. To the faithful, Advent is trusting in the slow work of God, knowing that the process *is* the path. In Advent, all that transpires is significant. With steadfast hope, we move toward the arrival of Emmanuel: God with us. We see him, though not yet. We behold him, though not near. O come, o come, Emmanuel.

Numbers 24:2–7,15–17a
Psalm 25:4–5ab,6 and 7bc,8–9
Matthew 21:23–27

DECEMBER 17

*The book of the genealogy of Jesus Christ,
the son of David, the son of Abraham.*
—MATTHEW 1:1

Of the four Gospels, Matthew's is the only one to open with
a genealogy, connecting Jesus to David, and beyond. It is
more symbolic than historically accurate. But Matthew is
making an important point: Jesus descends from real people
in the Old Testament, the people of the covenant and the
promise God first made to Abraham. The birth of Jesus to
Mary and Joseph is the culmination of a very long story.
Jesus is the fulfillment of the promise God made to his
people centuries before, and God always keeps his promises.
This is what Matthew's genealogy reminds us.

Genesis 49:2,8–10
Psalm 72:1–2,3–4ab,7–8,17
Matthew 1:1–17

DECEMBER 18

And blessed forever be his glorious name,
may the whole earth be filled with his glory.
—PSALM 72:19

"The Advent season is a time of preparation that directs our hearts and minds to Christ's second coming at the end of time and to the anniversary of Our Lord's birth on Christmas. . . . Advent is not about speculation. Our Advent readings call us to be alert and ready, not weighted down and distracted by the cares of this world (Luke 21:34–36). . . . Advent also includes an element of penance in the sense of preparing, quieting, and disciplining our hearts for the full joy of Christmas." *From* the United States Conference of Catholic Bishops

Jeremiah 23:5–8
Psalm 72:1–2,12–13,18–19
Matthew 1:18–25

Thursday

DECEMBER 19

The woman went and told her husband,
"A man of God came to me;
he had the appearance of an angel of God, terrible indeed.
I did not ask him where he came from, nor did he tell me his name.
But he said to me,
"You will be with child and will bear a son."'
—JUDGES 13:6–7A

The church chooses this Advent reading to highlight the similarities between the birth of Samson and that of Jesus because it speaks to the deep longing of the people of Israel for the Messiah. "When the Church celebrates the liturgy of Advent each year, she makes present this ancient expectancy of the Messiah, for by sharing in the long preparation for the Savior's first coming, the faithful renew their ardent desire for his second coming" (*Catechism of the Catholic Church* no. 524).

Judges 13:2–7,24–25a
Psalm 71:3–4a,5–6ab,16–17
Luke 1:5–25

Therefore the Lord himself will give you this sign:
the virgin shall conceive and bear a son,
and shall name him Emmanuel.
—ISAIAH 7:14

The Old Testament predicts the birth of Jesus many times.
But nowhere do the references sound more accurate than in
Isaiah. The prophet makes nearly a dozen predictions about
the coming Messiah. The church carefully chooses our
Advent readings to highlight the relationship between the
Old and New Testaments. Because, rather than two separate
books, the Bible is one long book, one long story with two
major sections. It is the story of God and his people. It has a
beginning and a middle, and we are still living the final
chapter. Advent is the beginning of the ending.

Isaiah 7:10–14
Psalm 24:1–2,3–4ab,5–6
Luke 1:26–38

• ST. PETER CANISIUS, PRIEST AND DOCTOR OF THE CHURCH •

The LORD, your God, is in your midst,
a mighty savior;
He will rejoice over you with gladness,
and renew you in his love,
He will sing joyfully because of you.
—ZEPHANIAH 3:17

In all our Advent preparation of prayer, penance, and petition, we cannot forget to celebrate. Christmas celebrates God in our midst. The bridge between heaven and earth was opened, and God walked across it bearing in his arms his beloved son. He gave us the greatest gift he could offer, our Redeemer. So, yes, Advent is a time of preparation, but it's also a time of celebration, a time of rejoicing, a time of love, a time of singing joyfully with our God for what he has done for us.

Song of Songs 2:8–14 or Zephaniah 3:14–18a
Psalm 33:2–3,11–12,20–21
Luke 1:39–45

*By this "will," we have been consecrated
through the offering of the body of Jesus Christ once for all.*
—HEBREWS 10:10

God made a covenant with his chosen people through
Abraham, and then with Moses, and Joshua, and then David.
Each covenant had its own terms to be fulfilled, including
animal sacrifices, rituals, circumcision, and other promises
made. The final covenant is Jesus. There are no more
covenants, no more sacrifices; Jesus is the final-and-forever
sacrifice. While God spared Abraham from sacrificing Isaac,
he did not spare his own son, Jesus. Jesus accomplished what
no other covenant did before him. Jesus is God's divine plan
of redemption revealed to us, and all that's required of us is
that we believe.

Micah 5:1–4a
Psalm 80:2–3,15–16,18–19 (4)
Hebrews 10:5–10
Luke 1:39–45

The friendship of the LORD is with those who fear him,
and his covenant, for their instruction.
—PSALM 25:14

"Fear of the Lord" in Scripture does not mean being afraid.
That makes no sense when we consider that God is our
Father, who created us and loves us. So, what does fear of the
Lord mean? It can mean a sense of reverence and awe for the
power and majesty of God. It can be a reminder—subtle or
stark—that we've gotten off track and God is calling us back
to right living. It can be the desolation of feeling a life
without the love of the Lord. The fear of the Lord can be
many things, but, unlike fear as the world knows it, all of
them proceed from love.

Malachi 3:1–4,23–24
Psalm 25:4–5ab,8–9,10 and 14
Luke 1:57–66

DECEMBER 24

"In the tender compassion of our God
the dawn from on high shall break upon us,
to shine on those who dwell in darkness and the shadow of death,
and to guide our feet into the way of peace."
—LUKE 1:78–79

Christmas Eve. Family. The shopping's done, the decorations are out, the tree has been trimmed, the presents bought and wrapped. Now there is the pause before Christmas morning. Holiday preparations have been exhausting, but it's the sweet exhaustion of what's to come rather than of what's been done. Let us remember that the greatest gift we can exchange is "the tender compassion of our God." We share it with ourselves and with whomever the holidays bring our way. This is how "the dawn from on high shall break upon us." This is Christmas.

2 Samuel 7:1–5,8b–12,14a,16
Psalm 89:2–3,4–5,27 and 29
Luke 1:67–79

Wednesday

DECEMBER 25

And suddenly there was a multitude of the heavenly host with the angel,
praising God and saying:
"Glory to God in the highest
and on earth peace to those on whom his favor rests."
—LUKE 2:13–14

Christmas Day. I recall my parents, who are no longer with me.
My children when they were little and Christmas morning was
a mad rush of torn wrapping paper. Now I look at my life—the
people, the events, the passage of time—and I'm deeply
grateful for another Christmas. God is good and I am blessed.

VIGIL:
Isaiah 62:1–5
Psalm 89:4–5,16–17,27,29 (2a)
Acts 13:16–17,22–25
Matthew 1:1–25 or 1:18–25

NIGHT:
Isaiah 9:1–6
Psalm 96:1–2,2–3,11–12,13
Titus 2:11–14
Luke 2:1–14

DAWN:
Isaiah 62:11–12
Psalm 97:1,6,11–12
Titus 3:4–7
Luke 2:15–20

DAY:
Isaiah 52:7–10
Psalm 98:1,2–3,3–4,5–6 (3c)
Hebrews 1:1–6
John 1:1–18 or 1:1–5, 9–14

DECEMBER 26

• ST. STEPHEN, THE FIRST MARTYR •

Into your hands I commend my spirit;
you will redeem me, O LORD, O faithful God.
—PSALM 31:6

We pray because somehow we know—despite all our
experience and knowledge—that we are quite helpless in the
face of the mystery of life and death. And do we ever
complete this life? Or is our life simply abandoned at the
time of God's choosing? I believe in the mystery of life but
not the randomness of death. God calls us when it is our
time, whether we understand it or not. Our task is to be
attentive, to be ready, to be aware, and when it is time, as
best we are able, to say the words of the psalm: "Into your
hands I commend my spirit."

Acts 6:8–10; 7:54–59
Psalm 31:3cd–4,6 and 8ab,16bc and 17
Matthew 10:17–22

DECEMBER 27

• ST. JOHN, APOSTLE AND EVANGELIST •

On the first day of the week,
Mary Magdalene ran and went to Simon Peter
and to the other disciple whom Jesus loved, and told them,
"They have taken the Lord from the tomb,
and we do not know where they put him."
—JOHN 20:1A AND 2

In John's Gospel, Mary Magdalene is at the foot of the cross when Jesus dies. She is also the first to discover the empty tomb. She tells Peter and John so they can see it for themselves. Later, Mary is the first person the risen Lord comes to. She was a witness to two of the most significant moments in Christian history: the Crucifixion and the Resurrection. While not one of the Twelve, it's obvious Mary had a special place among the first followers of Jesus.

1 John 1:1–4
Psalm 97:1–2,5–6,11–12
John 20:1a and 2–8

Saturday

DECEMBER 28

• THE HOLY INNOCENTS, MARTYRS •

Beloved:
This is the message that we have heard from Jesus Christ
and proclaim to you:
God is light, and in him there is no darkness at all.
—1 JOHN 1:5

St. Paul would say that to be Christian means to be Christ in the world. When we look at our world, we should see it with the eyes of Christ. When the world looks back at us, it should see Christ's face, Christ's eyes. We must be mindful of this. Our tone of voice, the touch of our hand, what we say, what we do—we are his presence, mercy, and love made visible in the world. There is darkness in the world, but for those who follow Christ, we must become the light in the darkness.

1 John 1:5—2:2
Psalm 124:2–3,4–5,7cd–8
Matthew 2:13–18

DECEMBER 29

• THE HOLY FAMILY OF JESUS, MARY, AND JOSEPH •

Beloved, we are God's children now;
what we shall be has not yet been revealed.
We do know that when it is revealed we shall be like him,
for we shall see him as he is.
—1 JOHN 3:2

We are the children of God from the moment we first
believed in him. But, like children, we cannot know
everything yet. In terms of the spiritual, what we know about
God, much remains a mystery. If we have faith, we know
there will come a time when all will be revealed and we shall
see the Lord as he truly is. Until then, we must love the life
we've been given, trusting God's promise of what will be.

1 Samuel 1:20–22,24–28 or Sirach 3:2–6,12–14
Psalm 84:2–3,5–6,9–10 or 128:1–2, 3, 4–5
1 John 3:1–2,21–24 or Colossians 3:12–21 or 3:12–17
Luke 2:41–52

DECEMBER 30

Yet the world and its enticement are passing away.
But whoever does the will of God remains forever.
—1 JOHN 2:17

The world is made of things that pass away, however
wonderful and sweet they may be. There is a temporariness
to all created things, and our world is tinged with the sadness
of the eventual. People and other creatures are born, live, and
then die. For those who do good works, those who show
mercy to others, those who care for others, those who show
compassion, and those who love—these acts may take place
in time but they also take place outside of time. Doing good,
doing the will of God, is how our souls secure our place
in eternity.

1 John 2:12–17
Psalm 96:7–8a,8b–9,10
Luke 2:36–40

DECEMBER 31

• ST. SYLVESTER I, POPE •

All things came to be through him,
and without him nothing came to be.
What came to be through him was life,
and this life was the light of the human race;
the light shines in the darkness,
and the darkness has not overcome it.
—JOHN 1:3–5

We now come to the end of the year. It is with gratitude that we look back and with hope that we look forward. The words of Ernest Hemingway can send us on our way: "It is good to have an end to journey toward; but it is the journey that matters, in the end."

1 John 2:18–21
Psalm 96:1–2,11–12,13
John 1:1–18

ABOUT THE AUTHOR

Joseph Durepos is the author or editor of several award-winning books, including *A Still More Excellent Way*, *Go in Peace*, and *No Greater Love*. He spent his long career in bookselling and publishing bringing a wide variety of authors and perspectives into the public awareness. Since his retirement, he is enjoying life with his wife, Mary, in Channahon, Illinois.